DIVORCE JOURNEY

CATHY R. HENDRIX

Copyright © 2019 by Cathy R. Hendrix

All references to God and the Lord are to Yahweh, the God of Israel and the Holy Bible. All scripture references are from the KJV, unless otherwise noted. All rights reserved. This book or any portion thereof may not be reproduced or used in any manner whatsoever without the express written permission of the publisher except for the use of brief quotations in a book review or scholarly journal.

First Printing: 2019

Paperback ISBN 978-1-7923-1539-8
Ebook ISBN 978-1-7923-1540-4

Executive Editor: Dr. Robert McTyre

YAH-Scribe Publishing, LLC
21627 E. 9 Mile Rd.
Saint Clair Shores 48080
www.yahscribe.com

Preface

Like most people, my life has taken some unexpected turns. At the age of 21 I married a man that I deeply loved. My commitment was forever, and I looked forward to the life we would have together. However, I would later discover that our commitment levels were not matched, and we suffered a divorce. I use the word "suffered" because, in my opinion, it is the most accurate description of what happens to husbands and wives who find themselves in this predicament and while your "day in court" may address your legal issues, it by no means absolves you of future suffering.

There is just something about the reality of your world, as you know it, imploding. The pieces of your life are no longer intact yet you are expected to keep living and functioning as if they are. I tried hard to keep it all together because I had very strong motivation – my children. The two people that I loved the most in this entire world needed me and therefore, my brokenness had to be "tabled" for a more convenient time. I did not allow myself to process the damage done to me in a healthy way because to do so would have meant an emotional breakdown and I had no time for that. So instead, I managed my crying spells and pity parties in a way that minimized the disruption to our lives.

As if it weren't bad enough to go through this once in my life, it happened again 12 years later. This time with greater detriment and impact because I was left alone with "myself" – no one else to care for and use as a much needed distraction. This is the experience that changed my life and led me down a pathway that inspired this book.

I felt the need to write this book because sometimes people believe that certain things do not happen, or better yet, SHOULD not happen to Christians. I have been a Christian for 37 years. I placed my faith in Jesus Christ as a teen and 23 years ago, became a licensed minister. This is who I am, and I live for Christ. Yet, it happened. Did I do something wrong or bring this on myself? I do not know.

Did I choose to love the wrong men? I do not know. Do I honestly know why the men I chose to love, and who promised to love me had a change of heart after many years of marriage? No, I do not. Although I do not know the reasons why, it is my reality, my story, and I want to share it so God can use this part of my life to strengthen and encourage others to "live again", even after suffering the worst experience of their lives.

Fast forward a few years, doors began to open. I was invited to Co-host a Christian Relationship Event called "Relationship Real", where I also served as a panelist for the divorce segment. After the event, women would approach me and tell me how they had gone through the same thing and how my words encouraged and uplifted them. I would pray with them for strength. I participated in this event for 6 years, making more and more connections with women.

It was not long before the Lord revealed to me that He wanted to use my experience as a means of ministering to broken women. He wanted to restore hope, demonstrate to them that they were still valuable, and heal their hearts. These are the things He did for me, and more.

Interestingly, as I would go place to place, preaching and teaching, there would always be an opportunity for me to share with the audience how God walked me through my "Divorce Journey" and transformed my pain into purpose.

Divorce is not a subject comfortably broached in the Christian community, nevertheless it does not discriminate. My experience has been that it is hardly ever talked about in church and very few have ministries focused on the healing and restoration of these broken Believers. I hope that my book will bring awareness to church leaders who may have never given serious thought to the emotionally wounded divorced souls in their congregations.

It is my prayer that The Body of Christ will realize that there are damaged brothers and sisters sitting on the church pews Sunday after Sunday who may feel like outsiders because they carry a shame that comes as a by-product of divorce. I hope this book not only brings awareness, but genuine manifestations of love, care and concern for the wounded among us.

In 2018, I started blogging, transparently about my journey through divorce. A following developed and an unexpected twist came about as I was encouraged to share the transformation that occurred in my life once I surrendered my will to the Lord's and laid my broken life at His feet. There are others like me, and I hope to lead you to, or introduce you to the One who can heal your heart, mind, soul, spirit, finances and emotions. Life is not over because your marriage(s) failed. However, it may be time to pull back and seek God like you never have before.

I also hope that those reading this book who have not experienced divorce will receive valuable insight into the experience that may assist in undergirding loved ones who may find themselves in this unfortunate situation. Divorce touches most of our lives in some way and perhaps the information in this book will cause you to develop a sensitivity you did not have before towards those reeling from this experience.

You do not have to be a divorcee, or Christian, to connect with my journey. You only need be someone who has suffered traumatic loss, devastation, hopelessness or heartache. I suppose you only need to be human.

I am not a credentialed therapist, psychiatrist, or doctor of any sort. I am, however, the most qualified individual to tell my story.

Today, it is 7 years later. I still remember the pain, but it no longer paralyzes me. I still remember the rejection, but the love of God overshadows it. I still remember the loss of material things, but they have been replaced better than before. I remember not having enough money, now I have more than enough and share with others. I still remember the dark pit I found myself in, but I have been RESTORED, REVIVED, AND REDEEMED all because I surrendered.

I thank Almighty God, Yahweh, for blessing me to write this book and for the lives that will be made better as a result of my testimony.

I thank my precious daughters who are the "apples of my eye" and who opened my heart to love in a way never known before I became a mother. Always "there", forever supportive.

I thank my parents and siblings for helping me sustain when things got bad.

I thank every person who was used by God to plant the seed of book writing in my spirit over the last 21 years.

I thank every person who sought my counsel, counted me as wise and let me know that my words came from God.

I thank my best friend of 40 years, who was responsible for connecting me with Yah-Scribe Publishing. I also thank my God-Sister who has loved and supported me in every endeavor for the past 21 years.

A special thank you to Dr. Robert McTyre for his professional editing services. Prophet Blaine and Linda Hunt for walking me through this process and making my dream a reality as my Publishers at YAH-scribe Publishing.

Finally, thank you for purchasing my book and supporting my efforts to help others heal.

Chapter One

A SYNOPSIS

For me, divorce was like death. It was the death of my marriage that left a trail of grief, devastation, anxiety and brokenness. I was not prepared for the "new life" that awaited me, and I had many struggles, setbacks and additional losses.

As previously mentioned, I have experienced divorce not once, but twice. No one could have ever told me that this would be my lot in life. I married young the first time, 21 to be exact. We had a fun-loving relationship and truly loved one another. We had two daughters, a beautiful home, good jobs, and what seemed to be all the ingredients needed for successful living. There came a time, however, when it became obvious that our lives were headed in two separate directions and our marriage failed after thirteen years. I thought after surviving our hardest hit in our 8th year together, we were home free. I never wanted a divorce, I wanted change. But when it became evident, after years of waiting, that he was not willing to change, I had to make the most difficult decision of my life. It is important to note that although I had to exit the marriage, I still hoped and prayed that he would "wake up" and re-commit to our marriage and family. I maintained that hope until the day we went to court.

The next three years, I would be a single parent to my precious girls. Parenting is not designed for one individual, although it can be done. It takes two because each one brings different strengths to the parenting relationship and are equipped, by God, to fulfill very different roles. However, when life throws you a curve ball, you catch it and run with it. I did not like or enjoy being a single parent because of the overload of responsibility that was meant to be shared by two parents. Additionally, children do not get the benefit of having two loving, responsible parents pouring into their lives and shaping their character.

The decision to marry again was not easy. This time, I had other lives to consider. However, I always knew that I was a wife and mother and I was happy and content in those roles. My second husband and I were both Christian ministers and served together in the ministry for seven years during our marriage. I was very confident in our longevity because he was 17 years my senior, soon to retire, and was ready to settle down. It just made sense, so I settled in and "exhaled". I thanked God for "HELP".

As fate would have it, after my children were grown and independent, my husband decided he no longer wanted to be married after 9 years of marriage. He filed for divorce. You may be looking a bit puzzled right about now, as I was. How do you just "decide" that you do not want to be married and exit? I will discuss this in a later chapter.

This book takes you into my 7-year journey of pain, suffering, loss and ultimate transformation and redemption. As you read, please bear in mind the number of years it took for me to progress from broken to restored. Divorce causes major setbacks in your life and for some of them, restoration can take years. There are no quick fixes and you must do the work.

Today, I am healed mentally and emotionally, possess a forgiving heart, free of bitterness, financially whole, walking in freedom, healing others through my testimony, earning a college degree, considering a radio broadcast and writing my first book!
Let me serve as a reminder to you of what can happen when the worst experience of your life is surrendered to God. He can astound you!

Come…let the journey begin.

Chapter Two

THE JOURNEY BEGINS

In March of 2012, I found myself in the most traumatizing situation of my life. Three days after my 9th Wedding Anniversary, my second marriage ended abruptly and left me in shock, confused, angry, and sick to my stomach. I had no idea that my husband was planning to leave me. As the Lord would have it, I stumbled upon information revealing his plan and confronted him. He did not deny it. I literally thought I was displaced in time or having some sort of out-of-body experience. It just did not make sense.

I know you may be asking how in the world could I NOT have known something was wrong? I did not say that I did not know something was wrong; I said I had no idea that my husband was planning to leave me. There is a difference. All marriages have their ups and downs, but ours was not a hostile relationship in any way. In previous months, I saw his demeanor change and I noticed him distancing himself and not being as attentive as he had always been. Although I had a suspicion of why he was acting differently, I deemed him to be more mature and chalked it up to the "ups and downs" of married life. Couples go through changes and none of us are "googly-eyed" over our spouse every single day. I felt no reason to worry or be alarmed as I figured we would get back to "normal" after a while.

As I reflect back, my marital confidence was rooted in the fact that my husband made a point of demonstrating to me that he was there to relieve me of some of the burdens I had been carrying as a single woman with a family. Before we were married, he stepped up and started assisting me financially, showing random acts of kindness and "being there" for me. I remember a conversation that occurred early in our courtship. He asked me to tell him about my financial situation. I said, "You don't want to know." He said, "Yes, I do." For a moment I thought, "Okay. He's either going to stay or run for the hills." I experienced an unexpected job loss one year after my first divorce and remained unemployed for a year. Things had gotten pretty rough in that year, but I knew I had to tell him the truth. I told him everything and his response was, "Okay. I'm going to help you." I could not believe what I was hearing. If he had said, my situation was a bit much to take on, I would have certainly understood that. He kept his word and during the course of our marriage, he continued to be a man that I could rely on and who was genuinely concerned with my happiness.

I mentioned earlier that I had a suspicion about the cause of his "change in demeanor". He and I had been ministers for a long time prior to meeting one another.

We decided to start our own church and the ministry went well for many years as he was an Evangelist and had a way of talking to people on the street, in the grocery store, or on the corner and leading them to faith in Jesus Christ. I did not have that gift. My gift was teaching and preaching. He was the Pastor of the church and I was the Co-Pastor/Administrator. As the years went by, he became jealous of the response to my preaching as opposed to his preaching. The members would even ask him if I could preach more often. This became a source of discomfort for us both. However, I had no control over the people's response nor their request to him for me to minister more often. This began to drive a wedge between us. Although I knew the "wedge" was there, I had every expectation that we would work through it. In 2010, after 7 years of pastoring, we decided it would be best to close the church. He was battling major health issues which required me to care for him. I also worked full-time and carried a great deal of the weight of the church. It was simply too much for me to manage. We offered to assist the members with finding new church homes and we set out to find a church home for ourselves.

There would be many challenges to overcome in our married life but, what we experienced in 2011 was by far the most serious and frightful event. In my opinion, experiences such as this should bond and strengthen relationships. I believed in my heart that if we could get through this, we could get through anything! I was wrong.

In April of that year, my husband was home alone, I was at work. He called me and I immediately knew something was wrong because he was out of breath and his speech was slow and difficult to comprehend. He said he was having a heart attack. I immediately, hung up and called 911 and explained the situation and gave them permission to bust the door down if necessary because he was alone. I worked 40 minutes away, so I called my daughter and parents because I knew they could get to him faster.

I did not have my car that day as I had dropped it off for a service appointment that morning and used their shuttle to get to work. One of my dear co-workers offered to take me to the dealer to get my car. She was extremely supportive. I got in my car and drove very fast to get to the hospital. When I arrived, I found him in the ER, in a room on a gurney, covered up, shaking and shivering as if he were in the Arctic cold. I walked over to the bed so that he could know I was there. He said, "I'm cold." There was a huddle of doctors off in a corner discussing his condition and necessary treatment.

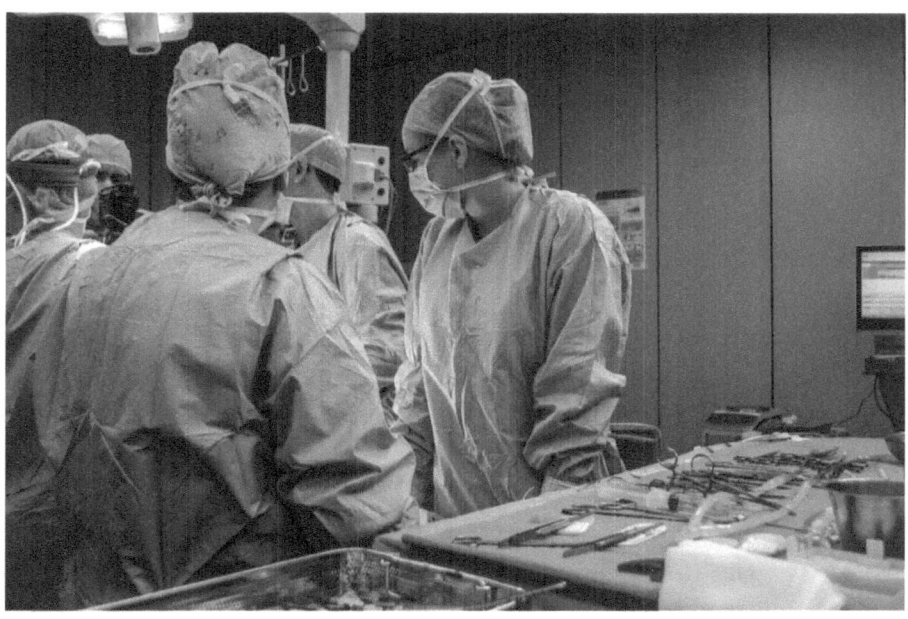

I could see the soles of my husband's feet, as they were not covered, and they were the color of blue. I noticed too that his nail beds were turning blue. In my opinion, he was dying.

This was the 3rd heart attack in his lifetime. I alerted the doctors and they did not seem to be moving fast enough for me. So, I took matters into my own hands.

I stepped into the hallway and looked up to Heaven and I said, "Lord, please don't take my husband. I'm not ready for this." I returned to the room and after a while, he started "calming down" and the doctors were attending to his needs. God not only heard my prayer, but He answered.

> **Psalm 46:1** – *God is our refuge and strength, a very present help in trouble. (KJV).*

That day, God was definitely my refuge (safe place) and my strength. He was present in our time of trouble and He was merciful. My husband received medical treatment in the ER and was transferred to a different area of the hospital.

Our next step was to see the Cardiologist for a consultation. We went to this appointment and were notified that there were 4 blockages in his heart. He needed a Quadruple by-pass. However, one of the arteries was too small and they would only be able to perform a triple by-pass. I cannot adequately explain the fear that gripped me in that moment. I was afraid that he would not survive the surgery, given his heart was so weak. He had concerns as well, but knew it was necessary.

The surgery was scheduled, and we had numerous appointments to prepare for the surgery. The day of surgery, I did something that I regret. I went alone. I had such a strong support system in place, and they offered to be with me, but I declined because I did not want to inconvenience any one. That was not a smart thing to do. Sometimes, you just need to let people help you and be there for you. There is a time for exhibiting strength, but there are also times of weakness even for the strongest of persons.

Before they took him back to the operating room, I held his hand and prayed with him. His son came up and joined me and I was so grateful he was there. The surgery took 8 hours. It was 4 hours before I would receive the first update. The sitting and waiting caused great anxiety. I called my mother after the first update and just hearing her voice made me want to cry. I felt an overwhelming peace. There is something about your mother's voice that can calm and soothe your very soul. I did not have to tell her how I was feeling; she already knew, and she spoke words of comfort and let me know that she was home praying. I felt a bit stronger after talking to her. I thank God for my mother's love and never-ending support throughout my life.
I needed her that day and I still do today.

When someone has a Conventional Coronary By-pass Artery Grafting surgery, he is placed on a heart-lung machine that takes over the function of both organs. This allows the surgeon to stop your heart temporarily (Harris, 2013). As you can imagine, this is a very serious operation. Arteries are taken from another part of the body and used to make a "detour" around the blockage, thereby "by-passing" the blockage. We were told his recovery would take about 1 year.

When the surgery was finally over, I had to wait almost another hour before I could see him. I was not prepared for what I saw. He was still unconscious and hooked up to so many machines, so many wires. Fluid was draining from his body. I wanted to break emotionally. The nurse told me he would probably not wake up that day. I sat for a while, prayed for him and decided to go home and try to sleep. I was exhausted as it had been a very long day.

He was released from the hospital a few days later and I was given instructions on how to care for him at home and how to treat his wounds. He would also receive visits at home from medical staff and a physical therapist. There were so many medications and so much information. To say I was overwhelmed would be an understatement. I needed help.

Philippians 4:19 – But my God shall supply all your need according to his riches in glory by Christ Jesus.

God answered my prayer by sending my husband's sister from Alabama to stay a week with us and care for him. She was a professional nurse and we needed her. I was able to relax a bit more knowing she was there. Not only did she provide her medical expertise, but he enjoyed spending time with her as well. Truly a win-win situation. She would be home with him during the day while I worked. Also, she cooked and cleaned. They enjoyed watching Westerns---or as I like to say, "Cowboy and Indian" movies. I thanked God for her.

This was an unforgettable experience and as mentioned, his cardiologist told us to expect his full recovery to take at least one year. After a few months, I could see signs of improvement. He could walk further distances without getting winded. His strength was returning, and I was saying "Thank you Lord! Now we will be able to have a normal life." My hope was restored. Little did I know, seven months later my world would implode.

As he continued to get stronger, I continued to celebrate! We were doing fine, returning to normal routines of him preparing my dinner every day, having coffee with me in the mornings and just hanging out on weekends. We found a good church that we were both excited about, the Romulus Church of God.

However, I was home sick from work one day and I noticed he was not his normal, attentive self. He had been spending an inordinate amount of time on the computer lately and acting emotionally distant. I was home again the next day and knew something was off with him. I heard the Lord say that in a few days, you will know what this is all about. You know how you can just sense something? I felt that I was going to have the answer to this mystery soon. I was not prepared for what I would discover, however.

I was lying on the couch and he was in the office with the door closed. I felt led to get up and open the door to the office. His back was to the door, so I opened it quietly, went in and stood behind him just close enough to see what he was typing on the computer screen. He never knew I was there. What I saw was devastating. I learned that he was planning to leave me for someone else.

It is amazing what happens to the mind when it is in shock. I told myself, "You didn't see that." But, I knew that I DID see that. I went back and sat on the couch staring into space. I did not say a word. When he came out, he asked me a question of some sort and I said, "Why don't you ask _____?" I used the name I saw in his email. He was stunned and began trying to explain how he didn't want to hurt me. I grabbed my keys and left the house in tears and went to a friend's house around the corner. I called another friend and she met me in the parking lot at Fairlane Mall. I also called my daughters and I do not remember the drive to Fairlane. My daughters put me in a hotel room in a nearby city and I spent that night with a pounding headache trying to figure out if "this" was real or not. My mind was playing tricks on me…I could not think straight. I was in shock. How could this be happening after all we have just come through? I was there for him, I stood by him. How could he do this?

I was so angry and disgusted. I could not sleep at night and could not think during the day. I functioned on "auto-pilot" and felt as if I were in some kind of bad dream. I never stayed another night in our home. He followed through and nine months later, a week before Christmas, I was standing before a judge in divorce court…AGAIN.

Chapter Three

EMOTIONAL UNREST

The days ahead would be the most difficult I would ever face. This was my second divorce and the feelings of failure returned, but this time, with greater intensity. I wondered, 'What in the world is wrong with me? Two failed marriages." It is interesting how I assumed responsibility for his decision by assuming something must be wrong with me. I did the exact same thing after my first divorce. I struggled each day to manage the emotional pain, mental anguish, and stress that had become my new normal.

I remember waking up one morning and not being able to move my body. I felt as if an elephant was sitting on my chest. I had to call off work because I could not function. I remember crying with an emotionless straight face. It was as if my body cried on its own with no help from me. Another time I was driving home from work and completely passed my exit to my apartment. I was headed to my former home that I once had with my husband. As I approached that exit, I realized what I did. I told myself, "Cathy, you don't live there anymore." I got back on the freeway and went to my apartment. "Am I losing my mind?"

It was not unusual for me to "talk myself through things." Life was very different now. The break-up blind-sided me, so I had no time to prepare myself in any way. I was at a huge disadvantage. I started to develop social anxiety. I am a people person and always took delight in getting to know others, but I was becoming withdrawn and did not want to be around people in social settings. I was embarrassed. I was a middle-aged woman this time around, not in my 30s with two children to distract me from my pain. For the first time in my entire life, I lived alone. I didn't know how to navigate my new existence. I was completely lost.

The fact that I survived my first divorce without a nervous breakdown was a miracle in itself. I had never had my heart broken before and when I got married I thought my heart would be safe, protected and cherished. It was, for a while, but not for a lifetime as I had planned.

The thing I hated most was the loss of control over my life's trajectory. In each case, my ex-husband decided what was best for him, without regard for me (and our children in the case of the first divorce) and left me to simply accept it and deal with the aftermath. I have to be honest, I entertained hatred briefly in both cases. I did not deserve to have my life destroyed, I just wanted to be loved. But, this is where having a relationship with God made all the difference. My feelings of hatred were swiftly addressed. I was not allowed to hate because that would interfere with my relationship with God and I certainly did not need to add that to my list of woes. Resisting the temptation to hate became a realistic battle for me. However, I fought that battle until it was no longer necessary.

The empty space created by the divorce felt as massive as the Grand Canyon. I started to feel a longing to be "near" God. I would go to bed at night with my open Bible across my chest. For some reason, that gave me comfort. Or, I would place it on the pillow beside me. It had been 25 years since I slept alone (before marriage and children) and I was not accustomed to it. I never really thought about the security I felt having my husband lying next to me. Now, I felt exposed. I felt uneasy and vulnerable and as a result, I developed a sleep disorder. I had trouble falling asleep because my mind would not shut down. I was anxiety ridden and uncertain about my future. There were other times that I could not stay asleep the entire night. Many nights, I just lay in the bed, eyes open, praying for daylight to hurry up so I could get out of the bed and out of the house. I had to resist the urges to call my ex and go off on him.

It seemed every area of my life now required an adjustment of some sort whether I liked it or not. I now lived alone, slept alone, ate alone, and returned home daily to an empty house. For the first time, no one was awaiting my arrival. "How did this happen?"

My family and closest friends were my strongest support system. They called and checked on me regularly. My mom called me every day to see how I was doing and showed love and support. If a day went by and she had not heard from me, she would call and leave a message asking me to call just so she would know that I was okay. She even invited me to come back home for a while until I could stabilize my life. I appreciated her offer, but I did not believe that was God's will for me. I sensed that He wanted this time alone with me. I was a member of a very loving and supportive church when this happened and the way my church family undergirded me was nothing short of amazing. I will share more about them in a later chapter.

I became depressed. I knew I was depressed because the only thing I felt consistently was sadness, and hopelessness. Ironically, I have heard Christians say that Christians are not supposed to be depressed. I never quite understood that line of thinking. To me, it was the equivalent of saying Christians are not supposed to get cancer or break their leg. Depression is an illness. Given a choice, I do not think anyone would choose to be depressed. Things happen to Christians and non-Christians alike. This is because we live in a fallen world because of the sin of Adam.

Romans 5:12 -*For as by one man's disobedience many were made sinners, so by the obedience of one shall many be made righteous.*

Being a Christian does not grant immunity from the ills of the world. It simply gives you hope and help from the Lord when trouble comes. Additionally, it gives the blessed assurance that the Lord is present and will walk with you through your trials. Christianity does not mean the absence of trials. Actually, it pretty much guarantees them. The Bible has many examples of the trials and tests of God's people. We should expect trials as a natural part of our spiritual growth and development.

1 Peter 4:12-13 - Beloved, think it not strange concerning the fiery trial which is to try you, as though some strange thing happened unto you: But rejoice, inasmuch as ye are partakers of Christ's sufferings; that, when his glory shall be revealed, ye may be glad also with exceeding joy.

When my first marriage ended, I did not seek help from external resources. I honestly believe that having my children strengthened me and gave me the resolve to fight my battles. Knowing that my daughters were depending on me and needed me fueled my soul and spirit each day. Although I was broken, I had to put my emotions on the back burner, get up, go to work, and keep moving for their sakes. As I reflect on both divorce experiences, I see significant differences in the way each impacted me and the way I responded.

I knew I would need help this time around. I found out about a biblical ministry at a local church called "Divorce Care". I signed up. It was a small group that met weekly for 12 weeks. This was not a "bash your Ex session". There was a prepared curriculum with applicable scriptures, videos on various aspects of the divorce experience and how it impacts your life, a workbook, and discussion period. The facilitator was a woman who had experienced this painful journey and she was able to connect with us in an authentic, empathetic manner. We are still friends today.

This group was very meaningful to me for several reasons. It built my self-confidence knowing that I was being proactive in helping myself. I learned that my feelings were a normal response to my experience. I learned healthy ways to process those feelings. I learned that God does not throw divorced people away or consider them second class citizens. I learned that my relationship status does not define me as a person and the most important relationship is the one I have with my Creator. But there was one verse of scripture from my workbook that stood out the most and became my greatest source of comfort:

Psalm 34:18 - *The Lord is nigh unto them that are of a broken heart; and saveth such as be of a contrite spirit.*

This verse reminded me of God's compassion and understanding towards the broken-hearted. In the days ahead, I would recall this scripture in moments of anxiety, worry, fear and sleepless nights. Knowing God was with me meant everything. No matter what I faced, I knew I was not alone. That is when a "shift" occurred in my journey to wholeness.

While it is very common for people fresh out of divorce to enter new relationships, I knew that was not the anecdote for me, although I did make an attempt after 8 months alone. It did not work out and I was not surprised. Some people rush into new relationships out of their fear of being alone. I understand that. However, knowing the "brokenness" that occurs after divorce, I recommend taking time to heal before connecting to another person. It is important to be whole and process your "baggage" or you run the risk of taking that "baggage" into the life of another person. Also, new relationships are a great distraction and confidence builder. We are designed to want and need love and companionship. However, if you have experienced a divorce, I strongly suggest that you take the time to figure out why it happened, what you would do differently in the future and above all, process your anger, and other emotions, towards your ex-spouse.

If you were the offended spouse, there is an obvious result that cannot be denied. Your spouse let you down. Anger is a natural response. Anger can become a very dangerous emotion if left unchecked. The greatest danger it poses is that it leads us down a path to unforgiveness. I will discuss my battle with unforgiveness in a later chapter.

My emotional chaos would continue for many months and it was not something that another person could help me with. It brought me to the end of myself. I could not get myself out of this place and I believe that is the way God wanted it.

I was 46 years-old and threw my hands up in surrender. I told God, "I need you." As I pen these words, tears are in my eyes. I remember my feelings of utter helplessness. My prayers changed. I went from asking God to avenge me to asking God to perform His will in my life and help me to cooperate with Him. I was broken and humbled. I gave Him permission to do what He wanted with my LIFE! I abandoned the driver's seat. It had not served me well. I knew that my prayers would be answered because all prayers prayed in accordance with God's will are answered.

***1 John 5:14-15** - And this is the confidence that we have in him, that, if we ask any thing according to his will, he heareth us: And if we know that he hears us, whatsoever we ask, we know that we have the petitions that we desired of him.*

Little did I know my shattered life would be the clarion call to NEW life and relationship with my Creator. It would also be the season in which I would learn more about myself than I have ever known. However, there were issues to address.

Chapter Four

THE ROOT OF BITTERNESS

When I got married in 1987, I married the funniest guy I had ever met in my life. He was not only a handsome soldier, but he was charismatic, and everyone was ensured to have a good time if he was in the group. During our courtship, he was very attentive, giving and enjoyed doing kind things for me. I remember one day he told me that he was going to take me shopping the next day and I could get whatever I wanted. I chose a Coach purse and I loved that purse. We enjoyed each other's company so much and I always felt safe and secure with him. After marriage, he continued working hard, saving money, paying the bills on time and ensured that his family's material needs were taken care of. He did this for thirteen years and I trusted him and could depend on him.

We went through so much together: Military life with its challenges of separation, working low paying jobs at the beginning of our marriage, living with relatives until we could stand on our own two feet, etc. In my view, these are the times that "make" relationships. We suffered together and after several years of marriage, God honored us and blessed us both with good paying jobs so that we could not only purchase our first home after ten years of marriage, but build our own home. We were incredibly grateful and proud of our accomplishment. I thought our worst days were behind us. However, a few years after moving into our new home, I would discover that his heart had departed. When I found out he did not love me anymore, the blow was crushing. It shattered my very core because my foundational belief about marriage was that it was to continue "until death do us part."

You cannot imagine the anger, resentment and betrayal that I felt, or maybe you can if you have also lived this experience. My marriage was an investment of my love, confidence, loyalty and time. I made deposits every day for thirteen years expecting a rewarding return on my investment. I dreamed of the days we would travel and enjoy each other's company, just the two of us, when our girls were grown and independent. I dreamed of the day when we would celebrate paying our house off. I dreamed of growing old together and enjoying our grandchildren. Divorce is also the death of your dreams.

All that I held in my heart for a later time in life, was snatched away from me and there was nothing I could do about it. I grew up with parents who remain married to this day, 56 years. They had their share of trouble and great trials, yet they remained committed. I do realize that my ex-husband came from a very different family dynamic. But I could not help but wonder what did life have to offer him that was so appealing that he felt his wife and kids were expendable?

I am not one to give up easily and up to the day we went to court, I kept believing that he would "wake up" and realize what was at stake and ask me if we could try again. I would have said yes because I loved him. Not only did I suffer the loss of my marriage, but my self-esteem exited as well. After my feelings of pity, bitterness set in.

As mentioned earlier, my second divorce was an utter shock. I was blind-sided and got the "wind" knocked out of me. I was naturally angry, resentful and wondered WHY did God allow this to happen. My second husband was a very attentive man and believed in providing for his family. My happiness was important to him and he would be very disturbed if he knew I was sad or burdened by something. He once told me that, "My job is to get those tears out of your eyes." He defended my honor and actually was a bit over-protective. However, he cleverly hid his own internal battles. When it was revealed to me his plans to leave, I instantly became bitter. Now, I am facing a second divorce. How much can one heart take?

I have known many people that have experienced divorce. Some never recovered and it has been over 30 years. Some moved on, but did they really recover? Others believed that the best way to get over a broken heart is to find someone new. I have found that the human soul responds in various ways to this emotional pain and devastation.

It has been seven years since my second marriage ended and one day, I took time to reflect upon my experience. I do that from time to time as a means of emotional housekeeping. What I mean is, I try to "guard my heart" against evil. It is so easy for anger and unforgiveness to set in, even after you have made a conscious effort to resolve them. I find that they continue to lurk, waiting for an opportunity to return.

My divorces left me extremely angry and bitter. Who wants to keep starting over in life? I learned that it is not healthy to dismiss painful emotions. It was best for me to process them because continual anger and bitterness leads one to a very dark place in life where eventually, nothing will seem good anymore. I admit that sometimes I just did not want to hear scripture. I knew it was right and would convict me of my wrong. I just wanted to be mad. But, having a personal relationship with Jesus Christ left no room for my anger to go unchecked. The Holy Spirit reminded me that it was okay to be angry, but it was NOT okay to allow my anger to lead me into sin (sinful thoughts, words and actions).

Ephesians 4:26 – *Be ye angry, and sin not: let not the sun go down upon your wrath:*

I cannot tell you how many times I violated this commandment. In my weakness, I allowed my bitterness to lead me into sinful thoughts and words against my ex-spouse. Night after night, I nursed my anger and did not seek to resolve it.

I saw the mercy of God at work in my life. Although I was in violation of His commandment; He still loved, cared for and provided for my every need. I did not deserve His blessings, but He chose to bless me anyway. Sinful humanity continually stands in need of the mercy of Almighty God.

I cannot recall how long it took me to resolve my bitterness. I use the word "resolve" because it was up to me to do something about my condition. I had to work through it by acknowledging and confessing it was there, agreeing with God that it was sin, and asking God to help me FORGIVE. I will talk more in depth about my struggle with unforgiveness in the next chapter. Oh, how I wished that I would just wake up one day and be whole again! Not so. My bitterness was used as an instrument in the hand of God to show me my own sinfulness, His mercy towards me, and my dependence upon Him to be free of it!

As I would sit and brood on the injustice done to me by my former spouse, God brought to my remembrance:

Romans 3:23 – *For all have sinned and come short of the glory of God;.*

In other words, "Cathy, you have sinned against me also." I could sense God saying to me, "What was MY reaction to your sin?" His reaction was to sacrifice His life to redeem me.

Romans 5:6-8 – *For when we were yet without strength, in due time Christ died for the ungodly. For scarcely for a righteous man will one die: yet peradventure for a good man some would even dare to die. But God commendeth his love toward us, in that, while we were yet sinners, Christ died for us.*

My thoughts turned toward the mercy of God. I have often defined mercy as "God bestowing upon us blessings we do not deserve." I had many bitter days. Yet, on each and every one of them, God preserved my life, provided for my needs, gave me the physical and mental strength to go to work each day and do my job despite my brokenness, and remained my constant companion. He would actually show me "signs" that He was present. For example, one day, I pulled into the church parking lot (a bit late!) and was prepared to drive all the way to the grassy portion of the back of the building to park my car. However, upon entering the lot, one of the brothers stopped me and greeted me. He said, "Sister Cathy, I'll park your car for you, so you don't have to walk all that way and I'll bring your keys to you." I was overwhelmed at this undeserved kindness extended to me. I knew God orchestrated this encounter to remind me that I was still "special" to Him. I needed that inspiration that day.

Psalm 103:8 – *The Lord is merciful and gracious, slow to anger, and plenteous in mercy.*

I realized that I could not rid myself of the bitterness that infiltrated my heart. I eventually came to the point that I wanted to be free of it, but it seemed to be so deeply interwoven in the fabric of my being that I was a "slave" to it. The remedy? I continually placed myself in a position to interact with God. As human beings, we generally turn to other human beings when we have problems in our lives. While there is nothing wrong with that, I learned that there are things in this life that only our Creator can help us get through. It is good to have someone to talk to and console us. God knows I needed my family and friends. However, they could do nothing to change my heart. It was my heart that needed adjustment, so I took action. I knew that although I had been wronged, I still had a responsibility to the Lord to do what was right.

I maintained faithful attendance at church to hear God's Word, attended Bible Study on Wednesdays, played radio broadcast teaching God's Word, listened to worship music that glorified God and I kept company with mature Christians who lived by Biblical standards.

Hebrews 4:12 *(CEB) – because God's word is living, active, and sharper than any two-edged sword. It penetrates to the point that it separates the soul from the spirit and the joints from the marrow. It's able to judge the heart's thoughts and intentions.*

One other thing, I removed television and internet from my home for 1 year! I had to take RADICAL action to uproot this seed of Satan that lodged itself in my heart. I refused to be distracted in any way and I committed to immersing my life in the Lord! I did not think I would survive without my TV and internet because there would be a silence like I have never experienced before. For the first time in my life, I lived alone, as if that wasn't scary enough!

Sometimes things happen to us that are traumatizing and devastating. It does not have to be divorce; it can be a number of things. Perhaps you have had to bury a child, spouse or parent. Maybe you were abandoned as a child, suffered abuse, or never felt loved. You may have been a victim of rejection, betrayal, or sexual abuse. Whatever it is that has crushed you, I hope you will take to heart the importance of facing it. More than likely, it will be excruciatingly painful and the very thought of it may bring tears to your eyes, but I am a living witness that you CAN get past it, but you will need God's help. Then, you can access a freedom that you may have never known before. What got me through was crying out to God, in complete honesty and BELIEVING that He was there and that He loved me even more than my earthly father.

Psalm 61:2– *From the end of the earth will I cry unto thee, when my heart is overwhelmed: lead me to the rock that is higher than I.*

Chapter Five

THE STRUGGLE WITH UNFORGIVENESS

The ending of my second marriage left me feeling completely alone for the first time in my life. My daughters were 12 and 13 years old at the time of my first divorce. It helped so much to have my girls as my focus. Their love and presence served as a distraction from the agony I felt when they were not around. Knowing that they needed me and loved me unconditionally allowed me to manage my emotional pain much better than I did the second time. This was the beginning of getting to know God in a way I could have never imagined.

I became a Christian at age 16 and was happy to devote my life to the Lord Jesus Christ. At this point, I was 33 years into my journey of faith. I was a licensed and ordained Minister, Bible Teacher & Preacher, Biblical Counselor and lover of God. However, I had no idea that God could take the worst experience of my life and use it for good. This will not occur automatically, but when ALL is surrendered to Him, He weaves it into a pattern for Kingdom good. This was a valuable lesson for me. So often, we expect the Lord to work out situations in a manner that results in our happiness and satisfaction. However, we must remember that His purposes are higher than ours. While he cares about our happiness because He is a good Father, His ultimate goal is the transformation of our lives into the image of His Son.

Romans 8:28 *(CEV)* says, *"We know that God works all things together for good for the ones who love God, for those who are called according to his purpose."*

I sensed in my heart and spirit that God was requiring me to FORGIVE before I could truly begin to heal. I earnestly told God, after an evening of emotional distress and turmoil, that I wanted to do what He required, but I just could not do it on my own. But, if He would HELP ME, I would cooperate with Him. Of course, I knew that a refusal to forgive would be outright rebellion and that was certainly not what I wanted. Some days the "heaviness" was so intense I felt as if I were dragging my own body around. There were times I felt as if I was functioning on autopilot. I was so numb that I couldn't feel anything. I wondered if I would ever be okay again.

Unforgiveness not only has negative spiritual implications; it also adversely impacts physical health. A study conducted by Johns Hopkins University entitled, "Forgiveness: Your Health Depends on it", states the following:

*"Chronic anger puts you into a fight-or-flight mode, which results in numerous changes in heart rate, blood pressure **and immune response** . Those changes, then, increase the risk of depression, heart disease and diabetes, among other conditions. **Forgiveness**, however, calms stress levels, leading to improved health.*

*Studies have found that the act of **forgiveness** can reap huge rewards for your health, lowering the risk of heart attack; improving cholesterol levels and sleep; and reducing pain, **blood pressure** , and levels of anxiety, depression and stress. And research points to an increase in the forgiveness-health connection as you age." (Forgiveness, 2019)*

Anger not only has an adverse effect on us spiritually, but physically as well. Releasing it contributes favorably to our overall well-being.

I recall one evening about 2 months after we separated. I was in my apartment sitting in my favorite chair having a conversation with God and I ALLOWED myself to feel the pain. I felt so heavy and burdened. It would have been easier to dismiss it, but it would not have been healthy to do so. As stated earlier, divorce is the death of a marriage. It is an indescribable loss and I believe all losses must be grieved. I cried from a place within my being that I cannot describe with words. It was a different cry – a wailing – an unleashing of something. I had never cried like that before and thankfully I never have again.

This is the day God spoke to me about the unforgiveness I harbored in my heart. I did not want to have this conversation because I did not want to forgive. I wanted to be angry and felt justified in doing so. I found that when you have the Holy Spirit living on the inside of you, He will give you a "moment" to process your emotions, but He will always do His job and convict you when you are wrong. (**John 16:8**).

> **Proverbs 28:13** - *He that covereth his sins shall not prosper: but whoso confesseth and forsaketh them shall have mercy.*

I knew that I was wrong, but I was so engulfed with anger and resentment that at times, I could not see past it. I had no idea how to even begin the process of forgiveness. God prompted me to SAY the words – make a confession of forgiveness out loud. I struggled with the words because I did not want to say them. But I said them. I – FOR- GIVE – HIM. I knew my heart and spirit did not agree with my words. Nevertheless, I obeyed. Every time an angry thought would come to mind, which was often, I would repeat my confession.

I agonized over this matter. There was nothing easy about this process and I honestly feel that it was one of the greatest spiritual challenges I have ever faced. There was just something within me that made me feel that I had some degree of power over my tragedy if I silently punished him in my heart. I felt that if I forgave him, I would be "letting him off the hook." He did not deserve to just "go free" after reaping havoc in my life. The inner turmoil at times seemed more than I could bear. I eventually decided to agree with God and allow Him to bring about the change that needed to happen in me. I certainly could not do it on my own. I surrendered.

Remember, we all have a choice. We can ignore God's voice in our lives, or we can submit to it. God gives free will. No one has to believe in Him or the Bible. It is our choice. However, each choice has consequences, just as it is in daily living.

I kept making the confession of forgiveness and I cannot tell you when it happened, but, in time, my heart and spirit aligned with my confession. I knew change had come when one day I realized that I felt lighter. I did not feel heavy, or shall I say, burdened anymore. My sleep became restful again. Joy and hope returned, and I felt encouraged. I was so incredibly grateful for the release. I am the type of person who keeps lists and derives great satisfaction from checking things off my list. I checked unforgiveness off my list – mission accomplished, and I do not have to worry about THAT anymore. Little did I know, there would still be a need to remind myself that he is forgiven. The anger would still come knocking. I would remind myself for years to come.

It is important that I mention that when God began to deal with me about the necessity of forgiveness so that I could heal, I had no apology from my ex-husband. Whether or not he took responsibility for his actions or apologized was completely irrelevant. Did I want an apology or acknowledgement from him? Of course, I did, and I felt he at least owed me that. But no matter what he did or did not do, I had a responsibility to do what was right in the sight of the Lord. It was my MY relationship with the Lord that was in jeopardy.

__Matthew 6:14-15__ - For if ye forgive men their trespasses, your heavenly Father will also forgive you: But if ye forgive not men their trespasses, neither will your Father forgive your trespasses.

As a flawed human being, I knew that I would need God's continual forgiveness and I did not want any barriers between me and the Lord. Sometimes you have to decide what matters most to you, holding a grudge against an ex-spouse or living the life God intended for you.

My testimony is that once I agreed with God and surrendered my will to His, He brought about the change in me that was so vital to my forward movement. Forgiveness freed me from stagnation and rescued me from the cesspool of anger and resentment. I did not realize that I had been the prisoner until I was set free. Now I was positioned to embark upon the transformational journey God had planned for me with nothing holding me back. It felt good to be free. Are you free? Or, are you nursing a grudge and refusing to forgive?

***Isaiah 40:31** -But they that wait upon the Lord shall renew their strength; they shall mount up with wings as eagles; they shall run, and not be weary; and they shall walk, and not faint.*

Chapter Six

REDEMPTION AND CODEPENDENCY

Redemption, by definition, is buying back, or repurchasing. It also means to free from captivity by payment of ransom (Redeem, 2019).

For the Christian, the redemptive price paid for our sin debt is the innocent blood of Jesus Christ, the Son of God, shed on the cross (**Hebrews 9:22**). We acknowledge that because of the sin of Adam, sin entered the human race, and everyone born after him was born in a sinful state, or, spiritually separated from God. Because God so loved the world, He created a plan for redemption to buy us back and release us from the dominion of sin over our lives thereby reconciling us to righteous standing with Him. We can partake of this plan of salvation by placing our FAITH (complete trust) in the finished work of Jesus Christ (**Ephesians 2:8**). To think, God did this because of LOVE. He wants relationship with us. Mankind is God's prized possession, the only part of creation made in God's very image (**Genesis 1:26**).

So, if I was already a Christian when I experienced divorce, why did I need to be redeemed again?

The redemption referred to in this chapter is not one of soul, but of mind. The Lord showed me that my mind was not in a healthy place and what I believed about myself and my identity was erroneous. I conducted myself, in my second marriage, in a co-dependent state. At the time, I did not know what it was, or that I was guilty of it. However, I have since been enlightened and the more research I did, the more I saw myself.

Codependency has often been associated with those who become enablers in relationships with addicted persons. You know, the person who makes excuses for her addicted loved one and refuses to confront when necessary and continues to protect him instead of allowing the natural consequences of his behavior to play out in hopes of teaching him to accept responsibility for his choices and actions. I must make clear that my codependent conduct was not related to a substance addiction issue. Continue reading for clarification.

In recent years, codependency has expanded to include those in imbalanced relationships where one person assumes a high cost "giver-rescuer" role and the other a "taker-victim" role (Manning-Schaffel, 2018). In plain English, this means an enabler or one who operates in a Savior Complex.

As mentioned earlier, my second husband had major health issues. He had physical restrictions due to his health, but the problems arose when I started to do things for him that he was able to do for himself. This was unhealthy for both of us because it deprived him of opportunities for independence in some areas and physical strengthening, and I was taking on responsibilities that were not truly mine and exhausting myself. Why? How did I become this person?

My best guess is that after my first divorce, the blow to my self-esteem caused tremendous damage. I thought that I did not "do enough" and maybe that is why my husband did not want or need me anymore. Therefore, my mindset was the total opposite as I entered my new relationship. I wanted to make sure that I did enough. Therefore, I began a destructive behavioral pattern of over doing that actually made me feel needed.

The problem was that the "give and take" was not balanced. I was not receiving to the degree that I was giving, and I was dismissing my own needs and not speaking up for myself. My perception of his needs was all consuming. I lost my voice and personally defined myself by how much I was able to "do". I honestly could not see the error of my ways while it was happening. It was not until the time of self-reflection came in my life that I realized this behavior flaw.

Learning the truth about ourselves is not always easy to accept, particularly in areas of deficiency. Who wants to admit that they have a disorder? I certainly didn't initially. But, as I continued to read and study the research on Codependency, it was undeniable, and I wanted to change. The first thing I had to do was change my mind and realize that I am nobody's "Savior".

You see, not much will change in your life until you change your mind. I had to go through a mental detox. I now know that things can happen to us that change us in ways that may not be evident right away. I am grateful that God helped me identify the "emotional crutches" in my life. I had to be de-programmed from low self-esteem, feelings of inferiority, and a Savior Complex. This would happen as I studied about my identity in Christ and replaced lies with truth. I decided to accept as truth what God said about me and allow these truths to govern every area of my life.

As I learned more about this disorder, suddenly, my life started to make sense. While I did not have all of the symptoms of Co-dependency, I had enough of them to sound the alarm in my consciousness. I would like to share some of those signs with you:

- Low self-esteem
- Low levels of narcissism
- Familial dysfunction
- Depression
- Anxiety
- Stress
- Low emotional expressivity
- Having a hard time saying no
- Having poor boundaries
- Emotional reactivity
- Always feeling compelled to take care of people
- A need for control, especially over others
- Trouble communicating honestly
- Fixating on mistakes

- A need to be liked by everyone
- A need to always be in a relationship
- Denying one's own needs, thoughts, and feelings
- Intimacy issues
- Confusing love and pity
- Fear of abandonment

(Selva, 2018)

Divorce led me to seek God like never before, and doing so allowed me to "hear" His voice. Hearing His voice revealed my Codependency and need for the redemption of my mind and identity. This discovery has been life-changing for me.

Today, I am aware of my tendency to "overdo" and have made necessary adjustments in my relationships with others. I am a much wiser woman as I have realized that everything is not my responsibility and every problem is not mine to solve. I have also realized the importance of stepping back and allowing natural consequences to play out so that others can learn and grow. In my efforts to be helpful and supportive, there were times that I was actually assisting the other party in negating their responsibility. I have learned that my needs are equally as important as those of others and accepting this truth has strengthened me as an individual and I am learning how to advocate for myself.

I had to establish boundaries and remind myself of those boundaries consistently. We are creatures of habit and it is so easy to defer to what is comfortable for us, although it may not be in our best interest nor the best interest of others. One of the ways that I learned to maintain balance was by asking myself a simple question. That question is "Can they do this on their own?" If the answer is yes, that means I do not need to perform the task, although I may need to facilitate. If the answer is no, I then need to decide to what degree do I intervene. Do I guide them through the process and teach them how to become self-sufficient in this area? Or, do I actually need to perform the tasks due to a genuine limitation.

I also learned that it is my responsibility to ensure that my boundaries are respected. People who will not respect your boundaries more than likely do not have your best interest at heart. I close this chapter by reminding you that YOU MATTER and while taking care of others, do not neglect taking care of yourself.

Chapter Seven

FINANCIAL LOSS

Financial loss is yet another devastating impact of divorce. In both marriages, my spouses and I were income earners and shared financial responsibilities. I was accustomed to living a certain lifestyle and after divorce, that changed and my only option was to learn to live differently… and do so quickly!

After my first divorce from my children's father, he paid child support. He was very responsible in this area and I knew he had a strong work ethic; therefore, I knew he would keep a job. However, it is not the same as having the full income of your spouse as a household resource.

After my second marriage, I was left with my income and of course, I had my share of the marital debt. We had no children together.

My husband, although retired, had been the highest wage earner and like most married people, we built our life on our combined incomes. At the time of separation, we managed to come to an agreement on our marital debt that was "doable" and I knew it would be challenging for me, but I was okay with the arrangement as it was fair to both of us. He had not yet taken me to court for a divorce. It would be 9 months before we actually went to court.

The problems arose about 6 months after our separation, when I found out he was not upholding his end of our agreement. There were dual financial obligations that still bore my name, that would be resolved when we eventually went to court, but were now delinquent and I was getting creditor calls. I had been so bogged down and focused on trying to pay my share of the marital debt that it never occurred to me to check and see if he was doing the same. I hope someone learns from my mistakes.

I found myself facing 4 lawsuits with threats of garnishment. Both of us were named in the lawsuits, however, because his income derived from a private pension and SSDI (Social Security Disability Income), it met qualifications for protection from creditors under the ERISA Act (Employee Retirement Income Security Act) of 1974. That did not mean that he could not be sued, but it would be next to impossible for creditors to legally collect from those income sources. Therefore I became the primary target as I was an active wage earner whose income could be garnished.

Now, I had a new set of problems – money and legal problems. I just wanted peace. I had finally managed to get to a better place emotionally and was trying to sort out my complicated life. Now this.

I recall being home on a couple of Saturday evenings, trying to relax, and there was a knock at my door. Once I opened the door, I was served. I could not believe what was happening and I had no solution. I was just thankful that these people did not show up at my job and humiliate me publicly. What was I going to do? It took all of my income to simply live and pay the portion of our debt that was rightfully mine.

As a result of this utter mess, I saw no other alternative than to file for protection via Bankruptcy. I did not see a light at the end of the tunnel. I was so embarrassed and ashamed of what my life was turning into. I had to borrow money from my parents and a dear friend in order to file for bankruptcy. How sad is that? The anger returned with a vengeance. But, I had to remind myself that he was forgiven. It is not easy for me to be this transparent, but I am convinced that you will not be able to fully appreciate where I am today unless you know where I have been.

As a result of the bankruptcy, my car was repossessed. I had to figure out what I was going to do for transportation. I had a bit of time before the car would actually be picked up so I prayed for guidance.

One day after retrieving my mail, I came inside and did a quick "glance" at the ton of junk mail in the pile. There was a letter from a car dealer in Sandusky Ohio advertising financing for persons in bankruptcy. Once you file bankruptcy, your information is available to certain creditors who seek to "help" you get re-established. Many are simply loan sharks that are looking to take advantage of you because of your financial situation. I was in the habit of just tossing these "offers" in the garbage. But, I felt I should read the one from Ohio. I decided I would call them and inquire. I had no hope that anything would become of my inquiry because my life just seemed to be on a downward spiral.

I made the call and decided that I was comfortable with the lady on the other end and felt she was very forthcoming. I was interested and decided to go to the dealer. They drove all the way to Michigan to pick me up. I was able to purchase a car that day, a beautiful Red Chevy Malibu that was a year old. It was in excellent condition and I drove home in disbelief.

Psalm 37:23 - *The steps of a good man are ordered by the Lord: and he delighteth in his way.*

I knew it was God that told me not to throw that letter away with all the others. After one year of timely payments, I was able to refinance the car and reduce the payment by almost 50% and significantly lower the interest rate. Things were getting better.

While my transportation issue had been resolved, I was still pretty strapped financially. It would take time to re-establish myself. I remember speaking to one of my dearest and closest friends on the phone one night and I just told her the truth. I was tired of trying to put on the "I'm okay" face when I knew that I wasn't. She let me talk and listened attentively and after my long rant, she said, "I'm going to help you Cathy." She did just that. On each of her paydays, she sent a check to me and she NEVER missed, not even once. My heart was overwhelmed and I saw her generosity as the hand of God reaching out to me to encourage me.

God reminded me of His commitment to Israel in **Isaiah 54:5(a)** - For thy Maker is thine husband. As an adopted Believer into the family of God, I decided to take this personally. One of the roles of a husband is to be a provider. God provided from a resource that was a total surprise to me. God also provided in another area, though not as surprising, but still so deeply appreciated.

I will be forever grateful to my daughters. When everything fell apart in my second marriage, they rushed to my aide and supported me in the worst moment of my life. They put me in a nearby hotel for the night so that I could rest. Afterwhich, my oldest daughter opened up her home to me and made sure that I was comfortable and made to feel welcome. I lived with her and my two grandchildren for two months before moving into my own place. She also helped me financially. God has blessed me with two amazing daughters. We have always been extremely close and we love each other very much. When one of us is hurting, we all feel it. We do our best to be there for one another and having them close gave me strength. I am blessed.

I remember a time when I paid my bills and I had $27 left for the week. I needed gas to go back and forth to work and I needed groceries. I had to think of how to handle this dilemma. The question was, "Do I buy gas or do I buy groceries?" I knew I could buy dry beans and some type of meat and eat that all week. So, I decided that I would go ahead and buy groceries and I managed to get food for the week and other necessities. I decided to trust God for the gas. I have very loving parents, children and siblings who would have happily given me money, but I had a problem with pride. I did not want to ask them. I just felt that my mess was not theirs to clean up and I especially do not like to lean on my children because after all, I am the parent. I borrowed $20 from a dear friend and co-worker. I was embarrassed to ask, but it was necessary and I knew that she would help me, no questions asked. When my parents read this, they will not be happy with me for not coming to them. There is nothing they would not do for me and they would rather suffer than see me suffer. I am blessed. I am just accustomed to being independent and if I have an alternative, other than going to my parents, I would rather do that first. I want to be a blessing to them all the days of my life, never a burden.

Like everyone else in the world, I had unexpected expenses arise and that just pushed me over the edge. A longtime friend and previous co-worker happily loaned me money for a particular purpose. When I met her to pick up the money, it was much more than what we agreed on. She said, "You're gonna need gas and food as well, so take this so that you have enough." I wanted to cry. She told me to take my time repaying her and not to worry about it because she was not pressed for the money. While her generosity moved me to tears, so did my shame of needing her help. I had never been in this "place" before and I learned humility from humiliation. I had no idea that God was at work behind the scenes building "Christlike" character in me.

What did I learn from all of these experiences? I learned that sometimes, we are so worried and afraid because we cannot see HOW a situation is going to work out. But, if we belong to Almighty God, He will provide for all of our needs just as He promised:

Philippians 4:19 *- But my God shall supply all your need according to his riches in glory by Christ Jesus.*

God uses people and His provision continued to flow into my life from unexpected places as I received unexpected financial gifts from family and friends. One Sunday, I went to church and my Pastor gave me an envelope. He said "This is not from me, but the person wants to remain anonymous." It was a crisp $100 bill. I was truly thankful as the timing of this gift was perfect.

One evening, I was at home on the couch and there was a knock at my apartment door. When I opened the door, there was a vase of beautiful red roses sitting in front of my door! There was no card and I saw no one. I never found out where they came from but the joy that filled my heart was invigorating. I love roses and this was truly a special gift.

A few times, I received the gift of a weekend get-a-way to Chicago from a dear cousin. She not only paid for my trip, but she took me on a shopping spree once I got there. These trips made such a difference in my life. It was an opportunity to escape my stressful environment and have a new experience. I loved taking the train because it allowed me to relax, think and enjoy the scenery and presence of God. Having my cousin to talk to and do things with was so much fun. She was so thoughtful and purposeful in planning my trips to her home. I will forever be grateful for her generosity.

When a divorce occurs and spouses go their separate ways, one or both of them can be left emotionally "bleeding and wounded". Financial and material losses were not the only set backs I experienced. I temporarily lost my self-esteem, confidence, identity, ability to trust, ability to sleep, and to have a sense of peace and dignity. As a wife rejected and abandoned by two husbands, I could not help but take a look at myself and come to the conclusion that, "It has to be me. Something is wrong with ME." I would later find out the truth, which I will share in a later chapter.

Thankfully, I have been restored in almost all of these areas by God's grace. My restoration came by learning who I was in Christ and it has taken years to overcome my negative self-image. It is very interesting to me how the people around me at work, in church, and in public, would compliment me in various ways and I would thank them, but I did not BELIEVE what they said because I saw myself differently. This taught me that the way you see YOURSELF is what matters most and what governs your life. There are people reading this book who do not have a healthy self-perception. I encourage you to address this area of your life because it can limit your potential, prevent you from taking necessary risks, and cause your gifts and talents to lie dormant. When we do not use our God-given gifts and talents, others suffer. God put in each of us what someone else needs and if you do not have the confidence to be the incredible person you were designed to be, someone else may not become the incredible person they were designed to be.

In this season of my life, I learned so much. God can move on the heart of anyone at any time and cause them to bless you. Do not make the mistake of limiting Him by a lack of faith. Everything belongs to Him so He is not short of resources to meet your need.

Psalm 24:1 – *The earth is the Lord's, and the fulness thereof; the world, and they that dwell therein.*

Of all my losses, one thing remained in tact: my relationship with the Lord. As a matter of fact, I learned to depend on Him like never before. My connection deepened, my faith grew and a new element was added to my walk with the Lord. I learned to "practice His presence."

Chapter Eight

SELF-TALK

I am going out on a limb here and I will say that we all talk to ourselves. Agree? The loudest voice heard each day is our inner voice. It is very important to evaluate what you are saying to yourself because your words have power.

In addition to my emotional battles, I remember noticing that I was developing social anxiety. This was very unusual for me because I have never been one that was afraid of public speaking or being in front of an audience for any reason. However, I noticed that I started feeling uncomfortable walking into a crowded room because I felt like EVERYONE would look at me and see that I was "messed up" inside. I felt as if a red bull's eye was on every piece of clothing I owned that said "DIVORCED - FAILURE!" In my own mind, I stuck out like a sore thumb. I was allowing the experience of divorce to become my identity and this was happening via my own negative self-talk.

Our minds are very powerful, and I discovered that this is the place where Satan launches his primary attack. In my own experience, it started with attacks on my self-esteem. As a woman, I was conditioned to give adequate attention to my appearance and strive to always look my best. When I looked my best, I felt my best. I considered myself attractive, but, because I was rejected, I began to tell myself that I must not be pretty enough and if I were, they would not have left. Yes, these were the words of a once confident, self-assured, strong woman of God. My conversations with myself became very negative, self-defeating, and antagonizing.

While I had people in my life that continued to bless me with their encouragement, positivity, and words of affirmation; I came to realize that it did not matter how wonderful everyone else thought I was because my own self-perception over-ruled their perspective continually. Something had to change and that something was my mind.

How did I change my mind? It took a conscious decision to change my mental diet. What was I "feeding" my mind? I was dining on persistent thoughts of failure, loss, and rejection. As I fed on this poison each day, my mind became contaminated and eventually consumed with this pollution. I knew that if I did not get this in check, the pollution would eventually defile my heart and if I allowed that to happen, my words would be next. God brought to my remembrance that it is my words that He uses to bless the lives of others. He has gifted me with words that can minister to the needs of the hurting, speak His truth, and impact lives. I began to see what Satan's goal was. He was after my words and he had a plan. But, Almighty God, revealed the plan before it could be carried out. Herein lies the beauty of personal relationship with Jesus Christ.

I started reading my Bible again, even when it was hard to focus and comprehend. I kept reading. I intentionally put myself in position to hear God's Word by going to church, listening on radio, YouTube videos, etc. As I remained committed to this task, God would lead me to verses that spoke to my identity. For example:

***John 1:12** (CEV)– "Yet some people accepted him and put their faith in him. So, he gave them the right to be the children of God."*

I knew that I had accepted Jesus Christ and placed my faith in Him, therefore I was a child of God. If I was His child, that meant I was privileged to share in the promised blessings mentioned in His Word.

My self-talk had to change, and I had to daily remind myself that God loved ME so much that He sacrificed His only Son so that by faith in Him, I could inherit eternal life in His Kingdom *(John 3:16)*. The negative thoughts did not just disappear, but I now had a spiritual weapon of warfare to do battle with Satan as he sought to overtake my thoughts and distort my identity. When negative, self-defeating thoughts would rise up, I would counter them with the TRUTH of God's Word and believe me, it was a mental war each day!

It took a while for me to learn to separate my experience from my identity. Divorce is what happened TO me, it does not define me as a person. There is so much more to me! I think it is critical that persons experiencing divorce realize that it was an EXPERIENCE and it is NOT the sum total of who you are. We must remember that our relationship status has nothing to do with our salvation. There is only one relationship that is paramount to our "adoption" into God's family and that is the one we establish, by faith in Jesus Christ.

If you are single, widowed, divorced, or married, you are valuable to the Lord. Every soul matters to Him and it is not His will that anyone should perish. Remember His words:

***2 Peter 3:9** - The Lord is not slack concerning his promise, as some men count slackness; but is longsuffering to us-ward, not willing that any should perish, but that all should come to repentance.*

I had to remember that God saved my soul as an individual and I was His child. I was His child long before I was a wife and mother and my marital status had absolutely NOTHING to do with my salvation. I had to be reminded that God loved me with an everlasting love because He chose to do so even before I made the decision to accept Him as my Savior. He loved me first.

Romans 5:8 – *"But God commendeth his love toward us, in that, while we were yet sinners, Christ died for us."*

Even though I am a mature Christian and Minister of His Word, it took daily reminders and recitations of scripture to create a healthy thought process. I learned that whatever thoughts I gave preeminence, are the thoughts that would shape my own self-perception. This verse is true:

Proverbs 23:7(a) – *"For as he thinketh in his heart, so is he:…"*

If you are in the midst of this horrific experience or are still struggling from a previous divorce, please know that it is your relationship and acceptance of Jesus Christ that gives TRUE VALUE to your life. I had it wrong. I evaluated my worth by my relationships with others, so if the relationship failed, I felt worthless. It is amazing to me as I look back to see how I completely minimized THE most important relationship of my life (with Jesus Christ), which had not changed at all.

Through the years, I have found a place of peace in my life. I no longer have the mental war going on each day. This peace did not appear overnight. Unfortunately, there is no "quick fix" on the pathway to peace. But, I know what changed me. It was my conscious decision to make the Lord my priority, not a new relationship, by spending scheduled time in His Word and praying to Him to "Please help me." He answered and I know this verse to be real because it is exactly what He did for me.

Philippians 4:7 - *And the peace of God, which passeth all understanding, shall keep your hearts and minds through Christ Jesus.*

My "Self-Talk" changed. Instead of rehearsing my pain, I created a new affirmation that was life giving. It goes something like this:

> "Cathy, you are a smart, compassionate, caring individual who is capable of empathizing with the pain of others and offering comfort and support. You are generous and welcoming and believe in treating all human beings with respect. You serve God by serving others with the gifts, talents, skills and abilities that you have been blessed with.

This is not a PRIDE session. This is me saying OUTLOUD who Cathy really is and embracing all that God has created me to be!

Here is my question to you: When is the last time you told yourself who you TRULY are? Or, have you taken the time to figure it out? Take the time. You will discover hidden treasure. When you find what is good, embrace it, say it OUTLOUD. It is okay to affirm yourself and recognize the beautiful gifts God has given you to pour into the world.

Your voice is the one that speaks loudest in your life and it is your responsibility to ensure that your "Self-Talk" is wholesome, edifying and TRUE.

Chapter Nine

LONELINESS

As mentioned earlier, for the first time in my life, I was living alone. I was not accustomed to silence in my home. I always had my kids, grands, or a blaring TV from my ex-husband when I came home from work. Silence was only something I could hope for. But now, I had more silence than I could bear.

It did not take long for me to experience loneliness. Actually, I think it started to surface the day after I left my home. I woke up in that hotel room and realized that I woke up alone, in unfamiliar surroundings. I did not have my husband anymore – my other "part" was missing. I was truly a fish out of water, and I had no idea how to cope with my feelings. There is a difference between being alone and being lonely. I was never alone. My parents, children, and close friends were always there for me. I could call on them at any time. However, I still felt lonely even when I was with them at times. My "special someone" was gone. I think we all need a "special someone" to pour our love into and share the journey of life with. God made us for companionship. From the very beginning of the story of Creation, when God made Adam, He said it was not good for him to be alone, so he made a suitable helper for him and said they are to become "one".

Genesis 2:18 - *And the Lord God said, It is not good that the man should be alone; I will make him an help meet for him.*

Verses 21:22 - *And the Lord God caused a deep sleep to fall upon Adam, and he slept: and he took one of his ribs, and closed up the flesh instead thereof; And the rib, which the Lord God had taken from man, made he a woman, and brought her unto the man.*

Verse 24 - *Therefore shall a man leave his father and his mother and shall cleave unto his wife: and they shall be one flesh.*

It was never God's plan for us to be alone so it makes sense to me that we would go through a time of grieving after the loss of a spouse or the "special someone" in our life.

I had some incredibly lonely days. It seems that Sundays were the most difficult for me because that was always "Family Day". My ex-husband was a very good cook and he would prepare wonderful meals for us to enjoy. I can recall moments when I would feel a wave of panic sweep over me as I anticipated Sunday. I would try to figure out what I was going to do because I knew that if I did not have a plan, I was going to have it out with loneliness. I formed a new habit of visiting my parents on Sundays after church and, occasionally, my grands would spend the night on the weekend.

Loneliness is a very "heavy" emotion. For me, it felt like I had a hole in my heart. I was used to being a wife and spent 22 total years in marriage. I did not have a clue how to live successfully as a single. But, one thing was for certain: I had to figure it out because I had no intention of continuing to feel the way that I was feeling.

My decision to remove cable and internet was not only a spiritual decision, but an economic one as well. When funds are low, you find ways to do things you enjoy in a cost- effective manner. I have always enjoyed watching movies. I like inspirational, drama, comedy and some action movies. I made good use of the free DVD rentals at my local library so I would plan a "movie" day for myself and decide what food would make me happy and then I would eat and enjoy a movie.

Social Media was very helpful because it allowed me to engage with a community of people I knew. Often, that was enough to comfort me, but that did not last long. I am a relational person and place great value on connections with others. I have always loved people and have a strong desire to help when I see a need.

As fate would have it, one day while at the library, I decided to take a look at the Community bulletin board. I saw a flyer for Hospice volunteer opportunities. I had never considered that type of service before, but I decided to give them a call. I spoke to the coordinator and we planned a time to meet so that I could find out more about available positions. In the course of our conversation, I mentioned that I was a minister. She was thrilled to hear that and asked if I would be interested in meeting their chaplain. I absolutely was interested so I met with her and discovered that she was responsible for a broad region of clients. She took me on as her apprentice and I went on visits with her for a short while and it wasn't long before she assigned me my own client list. I served as a Chaplain Assistant and this experience was life- changing. Ministering to patients at the end of their lives and the distress of their families truly put my life in perspective.

One of my patients loved baseball and the Detroit Tigers. He had baseball paraphernalia all over his room and that was all he talked about. It brought him such joy. He did not have dementia but had been battling cancer for some time. All I had to do was ask him had he seen any baseball on TV lately and off he went! Of course, the only thing I knew about baseball is that there are too many innings, the game is too slow, and I never wanted to attend one. But, it was a way to connect with him and make him smile, even if only for a short while.

I had another patient who was in the final stage of dementia. She was probably in her late eighties, did not move, respond or talk at all. She just lay in bed staring into space. I often wondered what she would say if she could communicate. I wondered what her life had been like. I am a deep thinker and analyzer and often like to get to the "root" of things. I visited her one day when her son was there.

He was about 60 years old. I introduced myself to him and knelt by her bedside so that she could see my face. I smiled and said hello. I asked how she was doing and told her how happy I was to see her again. I rubbed her hair and I asked her son if he would like to join me as I prayed for her. He did. I prayed for her and for him and then I asked how he was holding up. After that visit, I realized how much worse my life could be. I also realized that God had directed my steps to volunteer at this organization.

Psalm 32:8 (CEV) - *"I will point out the road that you should follow. I will be your teacher and watch over you."*

On the way home, I reflected on her "vegetative" state and realized that I was blessed to still have a healthy, coherent mother who knew when I walked in a room. She could talk to me, counsel me, hug me and smile at me. We could share a day together, go to the movies, out to dinner and if I just needed to lay on her shoulder, she was available to comfort me. She was the one person in the world who still got excited every time she saw me – with the exception of my toddler grandchildren of course. I was blessed. This woman's son no longer had his mother cognitively present. Her body was there, but she was afar off. My heart ached for him.

I discovered a remedy for my loneliness in the most unexpected place – serving others. Focusing on others takes your mind off of self. It is easy to get "stuck" in your pain but giving of yourself to someone in need will not only bless their life, but yours gets blessed by default. Service revitalizes the human spirit!

By the time I completed my service to the hospice organization, my thinking was different. I started to focus on the relationships that remained and not give too much mental energy to the relationships that are now past. I still had so many people in my life that loved, supported, and encouraged me. Both of my parents were still alive and well, my children were doing well, my grandchildren were the apples of my eye, I had great colleagues at work, a loving church family, and friends far and near. These are the relationships that mattered most, and I made a commitment to invest in them as best I could.

Holidays were difficult for a long time. These days had been the happiest times of my life, but for a while, they became the saddest of times for me. They were "special" but I did not feel so special. It would take time to look forward to holidays with joy and anticipation again. I remember one New Year's Eve, I cried and went to bed. But, I am so incredibly grateful that as time has progressed, so has my emotional strength. I do not dread any of my days, though some are more difficult than others. Nevertheless, I am alive, therefore I am blessed.

Chapter Ten

LEARNING TO BE SINGLE

One of the many challenges I faced was learning to be a single woman. The fact that I was middle-aged and had never lived alone did not help my adjustment to my "new" relationship status at all.

I had no idea how many areas of my life would be impacted by my sudden singleness. For example, I had to get used to no one being there every time I came home. I would return to an empty home that was completely silent…every single day. No one would be there to welcome me or ask how my day went. If I did not make it home, who would know immediately? There were days that I just needed a hug, but that was not possible. Prior to divorce, I was totally oblivious to the issues facing single adults. I now know how important it is to greet the singles at church, ask how they are doing and share a sisterly hug, or handshake with the brothers. Sadly, some people, that live alone, may go extensive amounts of time without physical contact from another human being. I encourage you to be mindful of those in your world who do not have a companion. Invite them over, call and chat, include them. You will add to their joy.

I had to get used to cooking a meal for ME to enjoy. I would no longer get the joy of sharing mealtimes with my husband. I had to learn to eat alone and appreciate the blessing of having food and the ability to prepare my own meals. This was so difficult in the beginning. You see, my ex-husband was a very good cook and because he was retired, and I was still working, he made my dinner every day. He also cooked on holidays when our family would get together for celebrations. He would cook and invite our church members over. So, a great portion of our life together revolved around food and connections to others. Now, I was eating alone. I could not bear eating at the table and would eat in the living room. Initially, eating at the table was just a reminder of who was no longer there to fill the empty seats.

I had to learn to enjoy my own company. This took some time because my life always centered on my husband and children. I hadn't really assessed what I like or enjoy. I realized my life was lost in the lives of others and I was downright boring! Now, the "others" had moved on, so I had to get a life and establish my own identity! Man… who needs this!!!

In order to discover what I enjoyed, I decided to be open to new experiences. You know, come out of my comfort zone. I found that I enjoyed movies (at home or at the theater), going to live plays/shows/musicals, taking vacations with my kids and grandkids, and sharing meals and conversation with friends.

During the week, I fared much better than I did on weekends. Monday through Friday, I worked so the majority of my day was consumed. However, weekends were torture for me in the beginning. It was during my down time that I would sit and try to make my life "make sense". It became VERY clear to me that I had to make sure that I planned a fun activity on my weekends. I also knew that I had to connect with people. There is no replacement for social connection. God designed us to need one another and I believe to deny that need is to inflict harm to the soul and spirit.

As I write this book, it is 7 years since my divorce and I still have to ensure that my weekends are planned, and I have something on my agenda that brings me joy. I also discovered that I like comedies! I will watch a "silly" movie just to make sure I laugh. Laughter is good for me. The Bible says in

Proverbs 17:22 – *A merry heart doeth good like a medicine: but a broken spirit drieth the bones.*

I feel that I have been very blessed in that I have not had many significant battles with loneliness. I know and have counseled women who resorted to one-night stands and made unwholesome connections because they could no longer bear being alone. I have had moments of loneliness, but, by God's grace, they have been few and far between.

Human nature presented battles of its own as I was learning to live as a single woman. I had never NOT had a relationship. I went from my parents' home to my first husband. There had always been a man in my life. I was a fish out of water and truth be told, our flesh always wants to gravitate to what is common and comfortable. I knew a relationship was the last thing I needed. Sometimes, we go from one relationship to the next as we try to manage our damaged emotions when what we need is to pause and allow ourselves time for wholesome healing.

There may be some reading this book who feel that you are ready to "get back out there" and meet someone. I encourage you to make sure that your self-esteem is intact before doing so. Divorce is a major blow to the self-esteem and if we are not restored in this area, we run the risk of accepting someone inappropriate for us. It is a good idea to have people in your life who are looking out for you. People that you trust to weigh in with their perspective on the person you are dating, if you feel it is getting serious. Women need men in their corner and men need women in theirs because men know men and women know women.

Being single put ME right in my face. I now had a very unique opportunity before me because for the first time in my adult life, I only had myself to focus on. I had a choice to make. I could spend the precious moments of my life wallowing in self-pity or I could seize this season and move forward! It took time to get strong, but I eventually decided to go forward. It is important to note that my decision for forward movement did not occur until my initial grieving season had passed. It would be two years before I was ready and capable of moving on.

Divorce forced me into self-exploration, and I am grateful for that. Because of this experience, and sincere soul searching, I realized that my dream of having a college degree was still present. I learned that I could feel wholesome and complete with God alone. I learned that I could be happy with a good video and a bag of chips. I learned to take risks and grow as an individual.

Remember, there is SO much more to you than what you have experienced! I gave control of my life to God and willingly submitted to His leadership for the remainder of my days. Best decision ever! COMPLETE surrender to the Lord has brought about a re-birth I never thought imaginable!

Psalm 32:8 (AMP) *—I will instruct you and teach you in the way you should go; I will counsel you [who are willing to learn] with My eye upon you.*

Chapter Eleven

PRACTICING HIS PRESENCE

As I have traveled this journey of recovery and restoration from the trauma of divorce, I have often had to just "sit with God." Sometimes, I had no words, they would not form, but I knew I had to be near Him.

The Center for Treatment of Anxiety and Mood Disorders, states the following:

"In general, trauma can be defined as a psychological, emotional response to an event or an experience that is deeply distressing or disturbing. When loosely applied, this trauma definition can refer to something upsetting, such as being involved in an accident, having an illness or injury, losing a loved one, or going through a divorce. ("What is Trauma", 2019)."

There are numerous ways of coping with trauma. As I have observed and counseled individuals after traumatic experiences, I noticed that no matter what their choice of coping mechanism, they adopted a behavior to "numb" the pain. For some that is drinking alcohol, for others it is immediately entering into a new relationship. For me, it was seeking God with my whole heart, all of me, and trying to get as close to Him as I possibly could. Naturally, I was tempted to just find someone else because the blow to my self-esteem was devastating. I understand why people move from relationship to relationship without actually resolving their issues. It is much too painful. It is easier to just move on and put the past behind you. However, my beliefs about marriage would not let me "step over" the fact that I have had two failed marriages. I HAD to know why this happened because if there was something in me that needed to change, I wanted to make the change. I needed to do all that I could to make sure that I never end up in this place again. Are there any guarantees? No, but it was important to me to learn as much about myself as I possibly could. I wanted to grow.

As mentioned above, trauma throws us into an emotional and psychological tailspin. It disrupts life as we know it, produces intense stress and anxiety, boggles the mind, and is not quickly overcome.

I am amazed that I have practiced Christianity thirty-seven years, but it was not until my life fell apart that I learned the power of "practicing His presence."

I define this as the deliberate habit of making time with God the first priority of each day by giving thanks and meditating on His goodness in your life.

I established a Saturday ritual. I wake up, have breakfast and coffee and then dedicate the next 2-3 hours to the Lord. This is a sacred time and those closest to me know that I do not take phone calls during this time. They know that if it is an emergency, they should call me back to back and I will know that I should answer. I have dedicated this time to hear from God and no one and nothing is more important to me. By making this decision, I am demonstrating to Him that HE is my priority and I will not give Him the "leftovers" from my day when everyone else has received my best. During our time together, He may remind me of a past problem that He has brought me through which invokes gratitude and praise, or He may bring to mind an area in my life that still needs healing which brings humility. He may remind me of something that I said that I should have said differently. But, most of all, He reassures me that I am LOVED and that He will always be there. Sometimes, I arise very early, before day, and go to my living room and sit on the couch – no worship music, no praying, no Bible reading…just sitting. I close my eyes and say "God, I am here." I have no agenda; I just show up. He meets me and I sense His presence around me, and the tears begin to flow. Experiencing God's presence this way is unexplainable. Once I have connected with the Lord, it is difficult to "leave". I started this practice in 2013 and continue to this day. I expect to continue for the rest of my life because I know how it has changed my life and contributed to my spiritual growth and development.

I am now trained to FIRST go to God when life gets difficult. When I am burdened, anxious, concerned or facing a trial; He has taught me to "sit with Him." When I am in His presence, the "heaviness" leaves. I receive strength and encouragement.

Psalm 61:2 – *From the end of the earth will I cry unto thee,* when my heart is overwhelmed: Lead me to the rock that is higher than I.

The intimate connection that I now share with my Lord was birthed through adversity. I did not know God in this way pre-divorce. It was my trauma that drove me to Him. For that reason, I am ever grateful for my trials because I do not feel that my suffering was wasted. It became useful and purposeful and pushed me out of comfort zones that birthed new challenges. I realized strengths and abilities that I never knew I had. I grew. We can turn to temporary fixes when life breaks us, but they are just that--temporary. After the euphoria of alcohol or drugs wears off, we are still left with our broken selves. After the sexual encounter with a new person is over, we are still left with our broken selves. These things do not truly satisfy the human soul and I believe that is because we are designed to commune with our Creator. There is no substitute for Him.

A temporary fix was inadequate for me. I needed a lasting result and God gave it to me. I needed to know He was with me. I have overcome many obstacles from the time of my divorce to the writing of this book simply because I knew He was with me. I did not need to know the answer or the outcome as long as I knew He was with me. I held on to His promise in every situation:

Hebrews 13:5(b) - ... *for he hath said, I will never leave thee, nor forsake thee.*

There were times when I was watching TV and God directed me to turn it off and sit with Him. This may sound strange to some, but when you cultivate a personal relationship with the Lord, His spirit dwells within you and it draws you to Him.

I mentioned previously that I went an entire year with no cable or internet. My testimony is that I grew more spiritually in those 12 months than I have in my lifetime. There are times when God will direct me to "shut in" on a Saturday and be with Him. He prepares the agenda by directing me to passages in the Bible to read, topics to study and guides my prayers. This is another way that I nurture my relationship with Him. Above anything else, I need HIM. He has assured me that I can handle what comes if I stay connected to Him.

John 15:4 – *Abide in me, and I in you. As the branch cannot bear fruit of itself, except it abide in the vine; no more can ye, except ye abide in me.*

Divorce left me broken and shattered. I was so shattered that I could not recover all the pieces of my heart. However, the beauty of serving the Lord Jesus Christ is that you can bring Him what remains. He is the God of resurrection and multiplication. He took 2 fish and 5 loaves and fed 5,000 men (multiplication) **John 6:9-14**. He called forth Lazarus from the grave (Resurrection) **John 11:43-44**. He is the same yesterday, today, and forevermore. He took the fragments of my broken heart and resurrected me to new life with a new heart. How do I know this? The evidence is that the anger and hatred that crept in when I was rejected, abandoned, and betrayed is gone. There is now forgiveness, love and compassion. I reached the point where I could pray for my ex-husband's best interest. I still do today. God is using my pain and testimony to bring healing, peace, hope and restoration to others. That is multiplication.

Oh, how I need Him. Oh, how I love Him. I don't even view my life the same anymore! This is because God pushed the "Reset" button and gave me a new mindset, a new attitude, new desires and ambitions – all to bring glory to Him!

Too often, we seek religion – legalistic practice of do's and dont's. I am here to tell you that God wants RELATIONSHIP. He does not just want you to know ABOUT HIM, but He wants you TO KNOW HIM, intimately. This is possible by "practicing His presence".

Chapter Twelve

WHAT ABOUT THE CHILDREN?

It was important to me, when writing this book, to be as thorough as possible in addressing the potential impact of divorce on children. They are the most vulnerable persons in a family and I sincerely seek to raise awareness about the importance of "tuning in" to your children during and after the divorce process. Naturally, there will be exceptions and not all children will have the same experience: however, as parents, it is still our duty and responsibility to be present and engaged.

My daughters truly surprised me with their response to our divorce. They were 12 and 13 years-old at the time and I just knew that I would have to deal with emotional rollercoasters and rebellious behavior that I was not prepared for. This made me quite nervous. However, to my surprise, my daughters were cool, calm and collected. They were not surprised to hear of our break-up. Sometimes we think we are keeping things away from our children, but they are so incredibly intuitive that the only person we are fooling is ourselves.

When divorce occurs, the primary focus is on the couple involved in the marital relationship. They are the ones who have the daunting tasks of "undoing" their entire life together while managing emotional shipwreck. They need all the support available to them.

However, it is critical to remember that if there are children involved, they are equally invested in the family relationship and also suffer loss. They are at the mercy of their parent's decision and may experience their own personal trauma, depending on the family dynamic and reason for the divorce or separation. Naturally, if there was an abusive environment, the spouse and children may feel a sense of relief after disconnecting from the abuser.

The Journal of European Archives of Psychiatry and Clinical Neuroscience conducted a study on children who experienced parental divorce before the age of 16. They did a 16-year follow-up to determine if there was a difference in the trajectory of the lives of the participants as opposed to those of non-divorced, two-parent families. The study result:

"Females from divorced compared to non–divorced families reported more psychological problems (higher scores in the Beck Depression Inventory, General Health Questionnaire and Psychosomatic Symptoms Score) and more problems in their interpersonal relationships. These differences were not found among males. Shorter education, unemployment, divorce, negative life events and more risky health behavior were more common among subjects of both genders with a background of parental divorce. (Huurre, 2006).

From this study, we see that the negative impact of divorce can carry over into adulthood and adversely impact one's life course. It is hard enough for adults to manage the devastation of divorce and we must realize that children are especially vulnerable to various types of fear and anxiety when their parents divorce because children's sense of security and stability is threatened.

There are many factors that come into play that affect how a child handles the demise of her family. There will be unique situations, but for the most part, children are often "in the middle" of Mom and Dad and depending on the maturity of the parents, they can suffer additional heartache and pain because of their parent's inability to conduct themselves as mature, responsible adults. Divorce brings out the worst in people and civility goes right out the window because there is so much anger involved. Generally, it turns into one big ongoing fight and unfortunately, children become yet another reason for their parents to fight.

Too often, children are used as "pawns" by one or both parents to gain control or leverage over the other. The best-case scenario for children occurs when the parents can come to a mutually satisfying custodial agreement, without having a judge, who knows nothing about their life or family, make that determination for them. However, couples are not usually able to do this because they are so caught up in the "battle" that their perspective and judgment is clouded by anger and the desire for vengeance. If they cannot agree, the court will decide and often times, one parent is granted physical custody, meaning the children live with them, and the other parent receives a visitation schedule. There is also the possibility of joint-physical custody where the children live with both parents equally. One parent may be granted sole custody, where the other parent has no custodial rights. There is also the issue of legal custody. Legal custody refers to the legality of making important decisions governing the children. (Custody and Parenting Time , 2019). This is where things can get complicated. As an example, in my divorce case, I was granted physical custody of my daughters and their father was granted "reasonable" visitation and joint legal custody. This meant that he and I had to work out visitation times and we felt that we could do that so there was no issue. I was supportive of his involvement in our children's lives and there was no concern of harm from him, so we were able to navigate this area of our divorce together. Since he was granted joint-legal custody that meant that I had to consult him for things like medical decisions and any faith-based matters that required a decision. Additionally, neither of us could take the children out of state without the other parent's consent. Now let's think about that. Under these guidelines, if he wanted to take the kids on a family vacation to visit his relatives out of state, I had to consent. If I wanted to take the kids to Cedar Point, he had to consent. He and I were blessed to be amicable to one another, but what about the bitter couple? They are so mad that no matter what the other parent presents, they have already decided that their answer is going to be NO! They are not focused on the impact to their children, they are focused on fighting their ex-spouse and if using the children is a means to "get back at them", so be it. I do not have to tell you what this does to the children. Too often, the non-cooperative parent thinks he is punishing the ex, when in reality, all he is doing is causing the children to resent him. I hope that those reading this book who are living this type of drama will re-evaluate their conduct. Your children are watching, and they are so much smarter than you think. I realize you may be suffering and hurting, but you must realize that you are setting an example for your children. If your words and actions demonstrate anger, you are planting seeds of anger in the garden of your children's hearts. If you plant anger, you will reap a harvest of anger. The thing about a seed is that it sprouts much later after it is planted, and it does not sprout as a seed but yields an abundance of what was planted. What am I saying? I am saying that you may not see the manifestation of your angry conduct in your children immediately, but it will eventually sprout, and it will present itself in a much greater magnitude than you could have ever imagined. The Bible has much to say about anger, but I will share this verse because I believe it drives the point home:

Ecclesiastes 7:9 - *Be not hasty in thy spirit to be angry: for anger resteth in the bosom of fools.*

While anger is a natural, normal response in certain situations, we must find a healthy way of processing and releasing that anger. I, too, battled anger. However, I also knew that I had to address it right away because it is like a poison to the human body. Take a look at this verse:

Proverbs 22:24 - *Make no friendship with an angry man; and with a furious man thou shalt not go:*

God has taken the time to warn us about connecting with angry people. If you are struggling with anger, for any reason, I encourage you to seek help. If you belong to a church, talk to your pastor or a mature christian. If you do not have that resource, contact a counseling agency or even ask your medical doctor for a referral. Determine that you are no longer going to live as an angry and bitter person because it is robbing you of the quality of life that God intended for you and it can negatively impact those around you.

Additionally, if you have realized that you have caused hurt or harm to others with your anger, especially your children, an apology may be in order. It is never too late to do the right thing, and remember: it matters less about how they respond, but what matters, is that you have taken the first step to healing.

Depending on the relationship of the newly divorced parents, children can be subjected to insults and put-downs of one parent toward the other. While a parent may have legitimate reasons for such feelings, she must realize that the children have a different connection to the other parent. Your ex was your spouse, but your ex was the children's parent. The child will NEVER see the ex-spouse through your eyes. Let them decide for themselves what relationship they want with their parent (*of course there are exceptions when a parent poses a danger to a child*).

There should be no expectation or requirement for your children to adopt your feelings and perspective about your former spouse. To impose such a requirement on children is a clear demonstration of the parent's maturity level, or lack thereof. I think adults sometimes forget that they are the one who chose their spouse. The children are a by-product of your union. Children are born with a deeply rooted connection to their parents and the parent-child bond is so intricately designed that I have trouble attempting to define it.

Why put this undue pressure on your children? In my own situation, I learned that children want to be loyal to both parents. They should not be made to feel that if they continue to love and adore their other parent that they are letting you down. Doesn't that sound a bit ridiculous? They need to know that they can count on your support in their relationship with the parent outside of the home. The dismantling of their family is hard enough but if the parents can agree to make the children's stability their priority, the children have a much greater chance of thriving at school, at home, and in the future. This also applies to un-wed parents.

If you must speak harshly and disrespectfully about your former spouse, find an adult friend who can handle that conversation. Please do not make your child your "friend". Children should never become a "sounding board" for adult drama. There must be healthy relationship boundaries between parents and children. In my opinion, dumping adult problems on developing young minds is both selfish and inappropriate.

Sometimes, incredibly selfish and immature parents try to "win" the loyalty of the child by bribing them with material gifts. Some parents actually compete for their child's affection by trying to "out do" the other parent. My perspective on this "parental competition" is that the fundamental foundation of love between the parent and child must be lacking. I say this because no one has to compete for what they already have. Additionally, when we try to make ourselves look "better" at the expense of belittling others, it speaks to an issue of insecurity. The children are better served by the parent establishing a genuine relationship with them based on love, trust and consistency.

Parents may use children to "spy" on the other parent and require a "report" once the child returns from a visit with the other parent. Or, one parent may decide to be unnecessarily non-compliant and refuse to obey court orders governing visitation. In this case, there will be additional legal proceedings costing more time and money.

Remember, no matter the outcome in custodial decisions, the end result is still the dissolution of the family and children having to adapt to a brand new life in two separate homes. They must remember rules at your house and rules at their second home and do their best not to get them confused. How often has a child said, "…but, Mom lets me do it!" It is extremely difficult to parent children who have healthy boundaries in one household and loose boundaries in another. Most children will "favor" the parent who lets them do what they want to do. If you are the more responsible parent, be prepared to not be on your child's "favorite person" list, they will thank you later.

Trying to get along with your ex may seem like the hardest thing in the world for you to do, especially if you have been wronged by that person. But, you are stronger and more resilient than you think and when you think of WHY you are being cordial and respectful to your former spouse, it should fuel you to press on! You are helping your child to feel safe and supported.

Chapter Thirteen

BLENDED FAMILIES

Oh Boy! This is a hot button because never in my wildest dreams would I have imagined that remarrying would come with such challenges. Of course, my experience is just that, mine. I actually felt relieved when I decided to marry the second time because from my perspective, now I would have companionship and help. I spent three years as a single Mom, and it was exhausting. I was the custodial parent and had all the responsibility of day-to-day life placed on my shoulders. I worked full-time, cared for my children, managed the household, searched for someone who could fix things when something broke, took care of car maintenance, hired someone to maintain the lawn, shoveled snow in the winter, went to parent-teacher conferences, shuttled the kids to medical and dental appointments, supported their activities, helped with homework, and we went to church twice a week since I was a minister. These are the things that I can remember; I am sure there's more.

No one has to convince me of the importance of having a two-parent household. I grew up in a very solid home environment with my dad and mom. My dad worked and my mom was a homemaker/entrepreneur/school volunteer. When my siblings and I came home from school, we had a hot meal prepared for us. We had structure and we certainly had discipline. Routines are important for children and, when you have a co-parent, it is much easier to implement routines because you have the mental energy to focus and plan.

Well, a lot of that went right out the window once I had the "full-load". I did my best with my kids, but I will admit, some things went lacking simply because I was mentally and physically tired, not to mention an emotional wreck. I developed a new respect for single mothers after I had the opportunity to live that experience. If you have never had to navigate this place in life, be grateful; and I pray this is something you never have to experience.

Okay, where was I? Oh yes, my decision to remarry did lift the financial burden of having to manage all the expenses of the household on my own. Also, my needs for companionship and emotional support were met. But I was blind-sided by the fact that my daughters were not ecstatic about the change in our family dynamic. This is something that divorced parents who are considering remarriage should evaluate closely. When it was just my girls and me, they could come in my bedroom at will, lay across the bed with me and enjoy free access to mom whenever they wanted. After remarriage, they could no longer do that, because it was no longer "mom's bedroom" but it was now a sacred space shared by my husband and me. Their access to me was no longer a free for all due to the fact that I now had a husband who deserved my time as well. My challenge would be trying to balance my time so that neither my husband nor my children felt neglected.

I really wish I had taken some kind of class like "Stepfamilies 101" or something because I was not prepared. My new husband joined us at our existing home, and these are the things I never thought about until they actually occurred.

1. He had never raised children so as a "new" parent, he did not know how to relate

2. He was 17 years older than I so our views on child-rearing were worlds apart

3. He was now the "head of the household" and thought the way to start our new family relationship was to ensure that everyone in the house knew he was in authority.

4. My children initially did not like him as "Stepdad", although he was okay when he was just dating mom.

5. I found out that having him over occasionally and having him around permanently brought out two totally different reactions in my girls

6. My children felt that I was no longer their ally and wasn't "standing up for them"

7. I often felt that I was "in the middle " of my spouse and my children

8. I did not know how to balance the separate relationships I had with my husband and my children nor did I feel especially skilled at "bridging the gap" between them.

Now that I am far past that season of my life, I can tell you that things got better. I do not know if things ever became "good", but they improved. However, I will say with all honesty, there was great difficulty trying to bring two worlds together that had no commonality and different expectations of how the relationship should go.

I have no idea who came up with the term "Blended" family because such families seldom truly blend. It gets especially difficult with older children. I know many people who have lived this experience and there is the rare occasion where it turns out to be a good fit. However, it can also become a total disaster very easily. Let me give you a couple of scenarios.

Think of the child who is broken-hearted over their parent's break-up. Often times, that child is privately hoping that their parents will get back together. Well, when the stepparent comes into the picture, they can be viewed as the one who "broke up" the family because now there is no possibility of reconciliation with the biological parent. The stepparent then becomes an object of resentment.

What about children whose parent marries someone who also has children? Not only does the child have to share their parent with a new spouse, but also with more children. They may now have to share a room with someone new or even relocate to a new city or school. Do you think they will be happy about that? These are just examples for consideration because I feel it is a very important issue and not generally on the minds of divorcees seeking their next "love" relationship.

Getting back to my experience, my girls grew to love their stepdad. I am not sure at what point their relationship changed, but it did. When our marriage ended, my girls were adults and on their own. Out of respect, they asked if I would mind if they maintained a relationship with him. Although my anger kindled against him, I supported their request because they needed him. He would call and check on them regularly and although he moved out of state, he would send gifts for the grandkids on birthdays and Christmas. He truly loved them and little did I know that the day would come when I would be glad he was there for them. Life is funny that way.

Their relationship continued until his passing in 2017. The girls and I traveled south for his funeral. This time, we were of one mind, one purpose.

Chapter Fourteen

HE DIED

My second husband passed away in December of 2017. I remember the day so vividly. It was December 14th and I was at school that evening. My phone rang (vibrated) and I saw his sister's name come across the caller ID. She lived in Alabama and it was extremely odd that she would be calling as I had not spoken to her in the years after our divorce. I actually had a beautiful relationship with all of his siblings during our marriage and although we were no longer together, there was never bad blood between us. I truly liked them, and they liked me and felt I was good for their brother. They were good, loving people.

I stepped out of class and answered the call. After saying hello, I heard, "Hi Cathy, this is Sally (*not her real name*). I asked how she was doing, and she replied, "Not too good. We found Bob (*not his real name*) dead this morning." I could not believe what I was hearing. "Bob" had relocated from Michigan back to the south a few years after our divorce. I was glad he went back south because I knew he was not a well man and needed the care and support of his siblings, who were all now back in the south.

I expressed my utter shock and gave her my condolences. She proceeded to ask if I might be able to help locate "Bob's" only son, who still resided in Michigan. Bob had one child from his first marriage. I told her I did not know how to contact him but would reach out to my daughters to see if they could help as they maintained a relationship with "Bob" after our divorce and may possibly keep in touch with "Bob's" son.

My heart was racing a mile a minute. "He's gone?" I just could not believe it. I got both my daughters on a 2-way call so that I could tell them at the same time. They were beyond shocked and so incredibly broken-hearted. They had come to love Bob as a father figure in their lives. When Bob came into my life, he fully embraced responsibility for me and my two daughters. It was a turbulent and sometimes painful ride as he came onboard as stepdad to his stepdaughters, but he helped them get their first cars, assisted with college expenses, helped support and babysit our first grandchild so my daughter could finish her degree and he just truly accepted them as daughters. It did not matter to him what their biological father did, or did not do, he always pitched in when they had needs.

The girls were able to locate his son and put him in touch with his aunt. I walked back to class and sat down in a daze. I was quiet the rest of the evening. I thought about notifying my instructor and just leaving class, but I felt I needed to stay put so things would feel "normal" to me. I always wondered how I would feel when "that day" came for him. When married to him, I was always concerned about him passing. I remember a day we went to his routine cardiology appointment. They told him he needed a defibrillator because his heart was so bad, he could have a cardiac episode at any moment and pass away. This was hard to hear and happened a couple of years before the need for heart surgery.

As I sat in class, I did not feel anything at all. I was numb. I wanted to feel, but I was numb. I was in shock for a couple of days. When the shock wore off, I began experiencing so many emotions at one time that I could not think straight. I had to remind myself that this was real. It really happened. He is gone. I thought about how he liked to cook and would cook my dinner every day. He would make us a pot of coffee on the weekend mornings and that would be our time to sit and talk. Then we would head out for the day to grocery shop, ride out to a rural area for a drive, go to a movie, or whatever we felt like doing that day.

Then I would think about how he broke my heart so abruptly and callously. How his abandonment and rejection sent my mind into a very dark place, my self-esteem to the gutter, and my heart....I do not have the words to describe my heartbreak.

Proverbs 18:14 (CEB) – *The human spirit sustains a sick person, but who can bear a broken spirit?*

Would I go to his funeral? Should I go? Is it even appropriate? How will I respond when I see him in a casket? Will I be angry? Will I feel love? Will I lose my composure? Will it be weird around his family? Oh my Lord!!! I cannot process all these questions. That's it! I am NOT going. It's over.

Whether or not to go was not a question for my daughters. They were going to bury their stepdad. They asked me if I was going and I told them I was conflicted. However, I did decide to go so the girls and I drove to Alabama. We were greeted with love by his family and this was my children's first time meeting his family. They included pictures of the girls and grandkids in the video of his life that played at the funeral home. That spoke volumes and I thought it was a beautiful gesture. I was not sure that attending his funeral was the right thing to do, but I felt that I needed to go, and many have told me that I needed closure. I will accept that.

Although he is no longer in this realm of life, I still think of him. I have had many conflicting emotional moments since December, 2017. I have grieved for him. I have still felt anger toward him, and I have rehearsed our marriage in my mind many times just to be SURE I did right by him. Although I know that I was a committed wife who loved and took care of him through many years of chronic and debilitating illness, I still had to reassure myself, at times, that my conscience was clear. I was so grateful that I had the chance to tell him that I forgave him. It wasn't just words, by God's grace, I was TRULY able to forgive him, but there could be no reconciliation. He asked on several occasions, but the breach of trust was too deep. I would never trust him again.

I choose to be grateful for the good that Bob did as he helped me through some very difficult times, stepped in to be there for my daughters, truly loved and cared for our grandchildren, gave to many in need and did his best to make me happy until he got off course.

I spoke about unforgiveness in an earlier chapter. I will say again, if there is anyone that you need to forgive, I pray that you will not delay. It is too important to "put off" until later and life is so uncertain; you may not get the chance later on. It is God's requirement and to withhold it causes God to have to withhold HIS forgiveness from you.

Matthew 6:14-15 (KJV) – *For if ye forgive men their trespasses, your heavenly Father will also forgive you: ¹⁵ But if ye forgive not men their trespasses, neither will your Father forgive your trespasses.*

Occasionally, I feel moments of sadness. I probably always will. But I have learned not to dismiss it or file it away for later. I have to "flow" through it, as painful as that is. For me, that is the only way to get to the other side of it. I give ALL praise to God, my Sustainer! I would have had a nervous breakdown by now if it had not been for the LORD who is on my side.

Divorce is the legal dissolution of a marriage. There is nothing a court of law can do about the emotional bond established between a husband and wife. For this reason, I caution others to think wisely before taking this step. There will be "residue" and while it may be a solution to current problems, it will bring with it, problems of its own.

Chapter Fifteen

THE POWER OF "I'M SORRY"

I'm sorry. These are two of the most powerful words in the universe, in my opinion. They have the power to heal and restore even the worst of situations when spoken from a truly repentant heart.

I remember after my divorce from my first husband, I wanted and needed him to apologize and take responsibility for his actions. I felt that would somehow make me feel better if he admitted that he was wrong. However, he did not, and since I have no power over anyone but myself, I had to accept that it was never going to happen. I resented him many years for this but as time and the years rolled on, I got over it and eventually stopped thinking about it altogether.

Fast forward 19 years, he reaches out and apologizes for his behavior, takes responsibility, acknowledges that he was selfish and only thinking of himself, congratulates me on all of my accomplishments and says he is glad the Lord put me in his life, and I am a beautiful person. Huh?

As I read his message on my phone, I could not believe what was happening. He said he was prompted to do this after reading a passage from my book that revealed to him how I was hurting during that time. I am not sure what he was referring to as my book was not yet published, but my guess is he read a post from my "Divorce is not the end" Facebook page. Nevertheless, his heart was moved and touched and so was mine. The flood gates opened and all I could do was cry, cry, and cry some more. Honestly, I am not sure why I cried like that. I no longer wanted or needed an apology from him after all these years, but maybe I did? Once I was able to compose myself, I felt as if that chapter of my life was finally complete. I had a vision of reading the last page of a giant book and finally closing the back cover saying, "It is finished." Oddly, I felt some type of closure where he is concerned.

Receiving an apology almost 20 years after an offense is a testimonial to me that God can do anything. I am not sure why the Lord allowed such a "delay", or even had it happen at all after all this time, but nevertheless, I thank Him. Additionally, I believe the Lord was demonstrating to me the impact of my words. To know that my writing caused a change of heart strengthened my confidence and conveyed the importance of my completing this work. My first husband and I maintain a cordial relationship to this day, and I will never stop praying God's best in his life.

It did not take my second husband quite as long to apologize. He soon realized that he made a bad decision. In a matter of a few months, he was calling me to apologize and begging for my forgiveness. I told him that I forgive him, and he thanked me. He then asked if we could reconcile. I explained that was not possible and he needed to move on.

An apology does not mean that everything will be restored to its prior state as that is not always possible. But for the offender, there is a sense of satisfaction in knowing you did what was right in the Lord's sight and made the effort to restore peace between you and the offended. In case you were not aware, seeking peace is a Godly act:

Psalm 34:14 - *Depart from evil, and do good; seek peace, and pursue it.*

Romans 12:18 (CEV) - *and do your best to live at peace with everyone.*

It is really hard for someone to ignore you or dismiss you when you come to them with a truly repentant heart. Even if they choose not to accept your apology, you have given God the "building material" He needs to work on their heart. Most importantly, you have pleased Him and something miraculous occurs when we please God:

Proverbs 16:7 - *When a man's ways please the Lord, he maketh even his enemies to be at peace with him.*

Is there anyone that you need to apologize to? Your "I'm sorry" could make all the difference in someone's life or future. Even if it doesn't change them, it will cleanse your soul knowing that you did your part to try and make things right. I realize there are offenses so grave that an apology will not alter the situation. But, as you read these pages, ask the Lord to reveal to you anyone you have wronged and make up your mind to put pride aside and go to them. I too have had to do the same. I have made mistakes and having experienced the impact of "I'm sorry" personally, I know that my apology can do the same for someone else. We are all human and we all make mistakes, therefore we will have many opportunities to say, "I'm sorry" and be used as an instrument of healing in someone's life.

Chapter Sixteen

SUPPORT SYSTEMS

When trauma enters your life, you will need others. There is no replacement for loving, supportive people who will listen to you, pray for you, spend time with you and be your "strength" at a time when you are weak.

While writing this book, I took the time to recount all the people that God had in place, and put in place, to support me as I went through my divorce journeys. As with any emergency or critical event, you have "First Responders". For me, this team was comprised of my beloved daughters, Chrystal and Carmen, my parents, sister and dearest friends, Kay and "Ms. Annette". They were in the "heat of battle" with me, defending me, covering me and attending to my wounds. They did not judge but did all they could to provide a safe place and comfort until the shock wore off. How blessed and fortunate I was to have them in my life and so willing to be there for me. All of them are still in my life today and God has blessed me to be there for them in times of need as well.

My situation was difficult for my parents. As a parent, I know how hard it is to watch your child suffer and not be able to alleviate their suffering. Parents are protectors and have a natural instinct to fix things and make it better. But in reality, they are bound by human limitations and when their child's heart has been crushed, they cannot repair it.

I recall during my first divorce, I had to pay my ex-husband his portion of the equity in our home since I decided to remain in the home and re-finance to a mortgage of my own. I did not have the cash available to satisfy this debt and my mom offered to help. Since this was a large sum of money, thousands of dollars, I agreed to borrow the money from her, and we negotiated the repayment terms. I lost my job almost a year later and fell on very hard times. My mom has always been an entrepreneur and she had a small business in a little shop at the time. It was time for a payment on my loan and I went by to see her one day at her shop and tried to be "normal". In a gentle voice, she said, "What's wrong?" She just knew and could see through my smiles and light conversation. I said "Mom, I can't pay.

I don't have the money." She said, "Is that what has you down? Oh, we can fix that! We'll just forget about it." I said "What?" She said, "Forget about it, your debt [of thousands] is paid in full." I was shocked and overwhelmed. That loan was never mentioned again. I write this with tears in my eyes although this occurred 18 years ago. She released me from a debt I owed but could not pay. She had every right to demand repayment, but instead, administered grace and mercy. Sound familiar? This is what Jesus Christ did for humanity when He released us from the debt owed for our sin by taking our place. He suffered loss so that we would not have to. What was His motivation? LOVE. What was mom's motivation? LOVE. She took my place and lifted my burden.

1 John 4:10 - *Herein is love, not that we loved God, but that he loved us, and sent his Son to be the propitiation for our sins.*

I was 46 years-old at the time of my second divorce and I was quite surprised at the degree to which I needed emotional support from Dad and Mom. Just being in their presence comforted me. I made a habit of going by their home after church on Sundays. I recall one particular Sunday where I was having an emotional upheaval and the entire day had been resisting the urge to cry. I went by my parents' home and no one was there as they had not come in from church. As I sat in a chair in their family room, I anticipated their arrival and every sound I heard, I hoped it was one of them coming through the door. Finally, Dad came in and greeting me with a hearty welcome, as he usually did, I started crying. I knew it was safe for me to cry "now". He hugged me and asked, "What's the matter, baby?" I shared with him a pressing financial matter that I was unable to handle, and he said, "Don't you worry, Dad is going to get the money." I knew he would do exactly what he said because that is the type of man he is. He hated seeing tears in my eyes and I hated having to tell him the truth.

I was very blessed to have the supervisors and colleagues that I had at the time of my divorce experience. I was working at a major university as an administrative assistant at the time and my supervisors were supportive, patient and empathetic. My direct supervisor was in utter shock and disbelief when I told her about my divorce as she had granted me personal leave time in the past to care for my husband during his illnesses. Ironically, it was April Fool's day when I told her, and she thought it was some kind of "joke" because it made no logical sense to her. My colleagues were equally stunned and equally supportive. I did not share with many people at work, as I prefer to keep my personal and professional lives separate. However, I had a few days where I just could not function and had to use sick time and I am grateful to have been supported and not reprimanded.

Chapter Seventeen

MY CHURCH FAMILY

My church community proved to be an invaluable resource during my hardest hits in life. At the time of my first divorce and subsequent job loss, my daughters and I were blessed to be a part of a local church in Ypsilanti called St. Mary's Missionary Baptist Church. I was a minister on staff there and the Pastor and congregation helped in ways that I shall never forget. They blessed me with money to help with living expenses, groceries, transportation, help with my kids, and household maintenance. There would be times that members would greet me in church with a handshake and slip money in my hand. There were times that they did not say a word but would walk up to me and discreetly put money in my hand. They called and checked on me. I did not have to ask, nor did I express a need. They were obviously led by the Lord as He answered my prayers through them. Their kindnesses were acts of "love" and this is how the Body of Christ should care for one another. They did not judge my situation, nor did they criticize, they gave. My prayer is that God will multiply back to them all they sacrificed on my behalf. They truly brought to life Ephesians 4:32:

Ephesians 4:32 - *And be ye kind one to another, tenderhearted, forgiving one another, even as God for Christ's sake hath forgiven you.*

The second time, I was the Women's Pastor at a local church in my home community, The Romulus Church of God, now called Kingdom Life Church. This situation was a bit different as my ex-husband and I united with this church as a couple and were in leadership. When he ended our marriage abruptly, I immediately notified my pastor's wife. My leaders were caring and compassionate yet stunned beyond belief. I was not sure how to handle the situation because we faithfully attended church and of course it would be obvious that my ex-husband is no longer attending and naturally, people would start asking about him. Also, I did not want to place myself in a position where I would have to respond to numerous inquiries.

My pastor inquired as to how I wanted to handle things and I told him that I would like to address the congregation. This particular Sunday, I stood before the church, microphone in hand and I said something to the effect of "My husband has decided that he no longer wants to be married to me and he will be filing for divorce. I wanted to tell you myself because I do not want the devil to use this as an opportunity for gossip or as a distraction. So, everyone has the same information." I do not know how my legs held me up or how I was able to say the words. It was God's grace. I made my statement with tears running down my face because I was both embarrassed and humiliated. What happened next was nothing short of amazing. As I stood up there, the women in the church began to get up and come down front to stand with me. They put their arms around me and around each other to form one big "Group hug". I felt so weak, but yet strong at the same time because I was drawing on their strength. After church, there were more hugs, not a lot of talk, a few "I'm sorry's". I remember one member in particular, a man, he said, "You'll let us [he and his wife] know if you need anything right?" I said "Yes.". And he added, "Even money." I said "Yes".

They gave money, invited me out to lunch, called to check on me, sent cards of encouragement and prayed for me. My pastor's wife kept close contact and continued to tell me that "God has a great plan for your life Sister Cathy." I believed her and she invoked hope where there was none. God had me in the right place because He knew I would need their support to get through this most devastating trial. I remained with this congregation four additional years before the Lord moved me on to prepare for my next assignment. Romulus Church of God was a place of refuge (safety) for me. It is there that I healed, was restored, and received the spiritual nourishment that I needed to continue growing. I was loved, valued and appreciated by a body of Believers that I still adore and have friendships with to this very day.

I have always been a part of a church community as far back as I can remember. My mother took us to church as small children, and I have maintained connection with my faith-based community all of my life. I never knew I would need them in this way, but how grateful I am that they were there for me. Some people wonder why they should "bother" going to church and there have been moments in my walk where I questioned the "significance" of going to church because I thought, "I have a personal relationship with the Lord. I don't have to be in church to pray and worship God." I have also experienced hurt in the church, as have many Christians. But I am reminded of the words of

Hebrews 10:25: *Some people have gotten out of the habit of meeting for worship, but we must not do that. We should keep on encouraging each other, especially since you know that the day of the Lord's coming is getting closer.*

God instructs us to "meet" for worship. There is power in unity and we are stronger together than alone. We receive encouragement and edification when we are together, of one mind and for one purpose. This is why attending church matters. We also grow spiritually as we are taught God's Word and apply it to our lives. In a perfect world, no one would suffer hurt or harm in the Body of Christ, however, we live in a fallen world where evil exists. We must remember that the Christian church is not a place for perfect (flawless) people. If that were the case, every church would be empty because flawless people do not exist. We all fall short in some way (**Romans 3:23**). On the contrary, it is a spiritual hospital, a place for those who have come to realize they are incapable of meeting God's standard of righteousness on their own and choose to accept the sacrifice of Jesus Christ as payment for their sins and thereby receive God's declaration of righteousness (justification) through faith in Christ.

1 Corinthians 6:11(b)- *…ye are justified in the name of the Lord Jesus, and by the Spirit of our God.*

It grieves my heart and spirit when I encounter people who have been turned off to Christianity because of the ungodly conduct of some Christians. If you have had this experience, I apologize to you. I am painfully aware of those who have presented themselves as "know-it-alls" and self-righteous "angels" who never do anything wrong and are quick to point out the errors of others. I must interject here that there are those who may not be mature in the faith who simply do not know any better. However, when you encounter a child of God, there should be evidence of a spirit-controlled life. Here is what you should look for:

Galatians 5:22-23 (CEV) - *God's Spirit makes us loving, happy, peaceful, patient, kind, good, faithful, gentle, and self-controlled.*

If a Christian has harmed you in any way, my prayer is that you will forgive them, realize they are human and not close the door on a relationship with God because of the fault of mankind. God loves you and wants you to know Him.

I also realize that a standard of "perfection" can be imposed upon the church by those outside of the church community. Sometimes, people have unrealistic expectations of the church. While I agree Christians should live life by Biblical standards, I also know that Christians are a work in progress and church members have varying maturity levels. People in the church are there to "work out" their walk with God. There is no mystical spiritual transformation. Consider this analogy of someone in therapy. There is an issue that they need help with and just because they go to the therapist's office every Wednesday at 6PM does not mean that others should expect their conduct to change immediately. It is a process. However, if they stay with it and implement the advice of the professional, their life will begin to change for the better over time. So, please, do not expect Christians to be "flawless" humans. That level of perfection has only been exemplified in one person, The Lord Jesus Christ.

I learned that the "hands of God" are His people. If you are suffering, I hope you will consider releasing your troubled heart to the Lord and sincerely ask Him to help you. I also hope you will consider visiting a local church in your community for support, or even just out of curiosity. If you do not find LOVE there, I suggest you continue looking. LOVE is the mark of God's followers. Jesus said in **John 13:35** – *By this shall all men know that ye are my disciples, if ye have LOVE one to another.*

God has people who will walk with you, so you do not have to walk alone. It was through the community of believers that God truly met all of my needs. (**Philippians 4:19**).

Chapter Eighteen

GET THAT DEGREE!

About three years after my second marriage ended, I began to ponder the question, "What do YOU want to do with your life?" I had finally reached a place of stability and felt strong enough to move forward. The previous years were spent in recovery and survival mode and I had no wherewithal to introduce anything new to my life. It was all about learning to manage and maintain financially, emotionally and mentally.

Now, I was ready to do something. I was tired of being in a low place and suddenly realized I was free to make whatever choices I wanted and, for the first time, I was in a place in my life where I only had to consider myself in my decision-making. I must admit, it felt strange to be so liberated. But it also felt good at the same time. The thought of going to college, again, came back to me. I have always had this desire throughout my lifetime and just when I thought it was gone, it would resurface. I had tried so many times in the past and never followed through or was inconsistent for one reason or another. At the time, I was a month away from my 49th birthday and absolutely terrified at the thought of returning to school. So many negatives began to sweep through my mind: What if I start and stop again? What if I don't do well? What if the roads are bad in the winter? On and on I went with excuse after excuse! It is interesting to me how God uses people in your life to say what needs to be said to push you in the direction He has for you.

I talked to my daughters and they were extremely supportive. I have a co-worker who shared her story with me about taking 10 years to complete her bachelors because of family and life responsibilities. Then, one day while at work, a professor from Eastern Michigan University came to our building to check on her student teachers and we started talking about school and she told me the story of how old she was when she got her degree. I could not believe what I was hearing. I knew it was my time and my season and although I was apprehensive, I decided to, as the expression goes, "do it afraid." I started researching various schools and landed on Spring Arbor University's Adult and Professional studies degree program. I decided to do a two-year Associate's of Science degree in Business. I figured an associate's degree was enough to satisfy my "bucket list." I made the call and something totally unexpected happened. The young lady on the phone had the exact same name, first and last, as my oldest daughter. As we talked further, turns out she actually knew my daughter from a college fair because my daughter was an Admissions Representative for Davenport University at the time. She made me feel so comfortable and reassured me that my fear was normal but could be overcome. I went for orientation and enrolled right away. I knew this was the right choice and perfect fit for me as it was a private Christian college, small class sizes, meetings one night a week, and the professors were business professionals themselves and many of them earned their degrees at mid-life and personally understood the challenges of adult non-traditional students like myself. I felt right at home! My self-esteem immediately escalated, and I just knew I was doing the right thing. Often, I was the oldest person in the class, but I saw that as a plus because I brought to the class experience and knowledge gained from 32 years in the work force. I started working at the age of 17 and had experience in corporate America, local government, public education, and higher education. I was able to contribute in meaningful ways. Also, I had the opportunity to socialize and make new friends. I was doing something meaningful with my life and the more I studied for school, the less time I had to look back. God told me that all He had for me was in front of me, not behind me. It was time to get up and live the life I was created to live!

I LOVED learning, always have, and I approached my studies with a commitment and dedication that wasn't there before. "What was different? I was older, wiser and at a different place in life. I spent so many years prioritizing the needs of others before my own, but now, I was committed to focusing on myself.

Best of all, between work, going to class, homework, ministry and time with family; I had a very full life! It is important to be productive. Notice I didn't say busy. We can be busy doing unproductive things. I became an excellent student and at the end of my two-year program, I had all A's and one B! Can you imagine how rewarding it was to see my hard work pay off with such good grades? The woman who was formerly shaking in her boots was no longer afraid! I felt empowered and began to believe that I was capable of even more. As a result of my success, I chose not to receive the associate degree, but to continue on to a bachelor's program in Social Work (BSW). I am currently a senior in my BSW program with a GPA of 3.8. You guessed it; I have my eye on my master's degree in social work (MSW). Who would have thought that the woman who only wanted an associate degree would be preparing for grad school in the near future?

Most times, I would be the first person to arrive for class because I went straight from work. My class was a cohort, meaning my "group" took all of our classes together through our entire program. We were joined with a cohort in Ohio via video conferencing. I took the liberty of learning how to operate the equipment in the classroom and at times would help my professors set up and trouble shoot if we experienced technical difficulties. Well, the Site Coordinator took note of my ability to assist and recommended me for a TA (Teacher Asst.) position at Spring Arbor. Confession: I do pretty well with software programs and can usually figure things out, but when I do not know how to fix something, I pray. I say "God, please show me how to do this." I live by this principle on my job and when counseling others.

At age 53, I now have a life plan of completing college and transitioning my career to a role as a Helping Professional after retiring from the University of Michigan. I am praying for God to direct me to the proper internship (required in my Senior year) that will lead to an employment opportunity that allows me to utilize my 23 years of Christian ministry experience and social work degree to help people with natural and spiritual needs.

It is never too late to do what you've always wanted to do with your life. I met with a colleague, who is also a therapist, and shared with her that I WISHED I had gone to college as a young person, but for some reason I just didn't want to. She said, "You weren't READY then and wouldn't have had the level of success you are experiencing now." She was right, I wasn't ready, although everyone around me wanted me to be. I completely understand everyone's expectation for me to go to college right after high school. It was the most logical train of thought considering my academic success up to that point. I could not figure out why I was so "anti-school" at that point in my life, but I knew it was not for me. Funny how the journey of life prepares us to become the person God intended us to be! That is what I feel has happened in my life. The worst thing I had ever experienced was not wasted, but God found a way to make it useful to not only position me to fulfill my dream, but HIS purpose for my life, which is ministering to the needs of the poor and those who are hurting and are lost in this world.

I cannot recount how many times I have heard, and recited,

Romans 8:28 (AMP) – *"And we know that GOD CAUSES all things to work together for good for those who love God, for those who are called for His plan and purpose.*

My tragedy has been used to direct me to the pursuit of education. A degree was always a part of God's plan for my life because I will need certain credentials and experience to work as a Master Social Worker. My social work education is teaching me about the various natural needs of humanity and connecting me to available resources designed to assist persons needing help. I am also learning client interviewing and assessment skills and the key ingredients to successful client relationships. I am absolutely intrigued by the course work and can see how my education "connects" to my 23 years of ministry experience that has always included an element of counseling and guidance.

At age 53, I am incredibly excited about earning my degree(s), the opportunities I will have to be of even greater assistance to others, and especially the doors that will open for me to be a "lifeguard" to divorcees. When they are without strength, exhausted from trying to stay "afloat" and about to go under, I want to be the one that jumps in to save them, pulls them back to safety, and resuscitates them. Divorcees do not have to drown in shame, humiliation, anger, and failure. You matter to your Creator and He has a plan for your existence. Please do not "throw in the towel" because your relationship failed. It is so hard to keep going when the wound is fresh, and it may seem as if you are never going to feel normal again. Trust me, I know. But, if you keep going and remain faithful to God, you will get to the other side. He will strengthen you. I am grateful for the opportunities that I have had to speak, teach, and counsel those whose marriages are failing or have failed.

I did not go through all that I have gone through for nothing. It happened, and it almost destroyed everything inside of me, including my will to continue on, BUT GOD. When I saw my broken life as an opportunity to totally surrender to Him. He took those fragments and put me back on the Potter's Wheel and made me again. He did not remove my pain and scars that resulted from my experiences, but instead, He changed my perspective and gave me a new resolve to be able to cope and most importantly, to see my life from His perspective.

Jeremiah 18:3-4 - *Then I went down to the potter's house, and, behold, he wrought a work on the wheels. And the vessel that he made of clay was marred in the hand of the potter: so he made it again another vessel, as seemed good to the potter to make it.*

Chapter Nineteen

A NEW SEASON HAS BEGUN!

As of March 2019, it has been seven years since my divorce. Seven has significant spiritual value. In **Genesis 2:2-3** we find these words:

"By the seventh day God had finished his work, and so he rested. God blessed the seventh day and made it special because on that day he rested from his work. After all the work of creation was completed, God proclaimed a day of rest. "

I share this because I can see parallels of this story in my own life. For six years after divorce, there was so much work to be done. God had work to do in me and I also had work to do on my own behalf. As I mentioned in my introduction, for me, divorce was like death. God had to show me that my life was not over and that what remained was still useful if surrendered to Him. I had to believe Him and trust Him and allow Him to resurrect my crushed and wounded soul one day at a time, one week at a time, one month at a time and one year at a time.

God taught me how to accept good and bad and how to slay my pride and allow my life to be used as an example to others to demonstrate that serving God does not protect us from the sorrows of this world, but gives us confidence in knowing that we never walk alone and we have help in times of need. I learned to trust God in times of lack. I exercised my faith in ways that I would have never thought possible. I held on to the scripture that told me that God would cause all things to work together for my good, even when I could not see anything "good" that remained.

I gained the confidence to own my story and not be embarrassed and ashamed of my experiences because they were the vehicle that drove me to His presence. Today, I stand as a woman who, by God's grace, has overcome much adversity

Psalm 34:19

Many are the afflictions of the righteous: but the Lord delivereth him out of them all.

I thank God for the life lessons that ushered me to humility, quieted my spirit, taught me to be still, drove me to God's Word and transformed my thinking.

God taught me that my primary confidence must be in Him and Him alone. He gives relationships and marriage as a gift to mankind to be enjoyed and to mirror Christ's relationship to the church, but its success rests upon the commitment of both individuals.

God taught me the value of cultivating and committing to a personal relationship with Jesus Christ. I do not mean ritualistic, religious routine. I am referring to a "bear all" relationship where nothing is withheld, all is known, and all is surrendered. If it had not been for this relationship, I do not believe my end result would have been favorable.

God taught me that what truly matters is what HE says and thinks about me. My own mind turned against me and fed me nothing but negativity consistently. But God reminded me of His power of redemption! He redeemed me from my own self-defeating thoughts and strengthened me in such a way that I did not have to turn to a premature, romantic relationship for validation.

God taught me that emotions are unreliable, misleading and capable of enslaving a soul that has not learned to master them. If left unchecked, they will lead us to paths that God never intended for us to tread. They cannot be trusted and should never be used as the basis for our decisions.

God taught me that a broken heart is a vulnerable heart. In times of emotional trauma, we must retreat to a safe place and guard our heart so that it does not lead us astray.

God taught me the importance of grieving every loss that I suffered – marriage, security, home, dreams, dignity and the ability to trust. It was important that I acknowledged and owned them because to suppress them would only ensure a future date with torment. I had to allow myself to feel every loss, deep in my soul and acknowledge my hurt, pain, and brokenness. God cannot heal what you will not face, and denial simply leads to depression and a distorted reality.

God showed me how He can take the worst situation of my life and use it as a tool to teach the greatest lessons that I would ever learn. He would use my experience to show me that I, too, am capable of unforgiveness, anger, and bitterness if faced with certain circumstances. Although I did not like the presence of these damaging emotions, I could not rid myself of them without the Lord's help. In this God demonstrated His sovereignty and my helplessness.

God showed me that with His help, I can forgive genuinely, deeply and without pretense. I can pray for the best interest of those who harmed me. I have counseled them, and I have helped them.

I thank God for the apologies and acceptance of responsibility from my ex-husbands. It has been meaningful and helpful to me as I have journeyed through my healing process.

Today, I live a new life that is filled with hope, new dreams, ambitions, confidence, accomplishments and most importantly, a clear sense of purpose and spiritual maturity that came by way of suffering. After 53 years of living, I know who I am, and I know why I am here. I am a woman who loves the Lord and whose primary desire is to live for Him and please Him by loving and serving others and declaring His truth through the teaching and preaching of the Gospel. I am compassionate and sensitive to the needs of others, particularly the poor, needy, overlooked and forgotten. This is why the Lord has led me to a career in social work. I attend a Christian college and a prevailing theme in my degree program is that "Jesus was the first social worker" as He ministered to the needs of the people in His day. He was not only concerned with their spiritual well-being, but He was concerned with their total well-being:

Matthew 14:15-17, 21 (CEV) - *That evening the disciples came to Jesus and said, "This place is like a desert, and it is already late. Let the crowds leave, so they can go to the villages and buy some food." Jesus replied, "They don't have to leave. Why don't you give them something to eat?" But they said, "We have only five small loaves of bread and two fish." Jesus asked his disciples to bring the food to him, and he told the crowd to sit down on the grass. Jesus took the five loaves and the two fish. He looked up toward heaven and blessed the food. Then he broke the bread and handed it to his disciples, and they gave it to the people. There were about five thousand men who ate, not counting the women and children.*

I receive great fulfillment in helping people advance in life and showing them what is good about themselves. Encouragement is a powerful tool. I know from experience. If it were not for those encouraging me during my book writing process, I would still have this project on the back burner waiting for the "right time". I want to see everyone triumph over their circumstances and, when I can, I want to help turn victims into victors. I am proof that not only can you survive your worst experience, but you can be an overcomer. There is a difference.

I heard a sermon at Living by Faith Ministries in Romulus, Michigan in May 2019 entitled "I am a Survivor." In this sermon, a survivor was defined as one who remained alive after an event where others died. It is easy to comprehend that definition in the natural sense, but I applied it to my life in a different way. There are people who "died" on the inside after divorce. They continue to exist, but life has lost its luster. They only do what is necessary and have stopped pursuing dreams and have abandoned ambition. There is no drive, but instead, they coast along through life because what happened to them drained the life right out of them. These are survivors. They are physically alive, but lifeless mentally, emotionally and spiritually.

Now, overcomers are people who have experienced equal devastation and loss. They grieved and suffered and thought life was over. But, at some point, they found the wherewithal to decide that they were going to keep on living, keep on dreaming, keep on loving and create the life that they want to live. I am an overcomer and it is my prayer that every survivor will be inspired to become an overcomer.

In this sermon, the pastor stated that overcomers find new meaning and purpose in their lives as a result of their traumatic experience. This is true for me. After my second divorce, I was invited to participate in a Chrisitian talk show event called Relationship Real. I was the co-host of the show and also the facilitator of the divorce segment. I shared with the audience from my heart about the pain and impact of divorce, but I also encouraged divorcees to keep going. I ended up co-hosting this event for six years. Each year after the show, I would be approached by broken and hurting women who wanted to share their story with me. Others would just hug me and say "Thank you for that. I needed that." Others would ask me to pray with them.

I also served as a featured columnist in a Christian women's newsletter called "SIS" for 10 years, which stands for Saved

Intelligent Sisters. My articles touched many lives and gave hope and inspiration to women around the world. What began as a local newsletter targeted for a specific group made its way outside of the United States as women would share it with those whom they felt could benefit from it. The newsletter ended up in the hands of a local radio host who invited me to her show. Although that did not materialize, as fate would have it, three years later my best friend encountered her at an event and inquired about her recently published book, and connected me with her publisher, who is responsible for the book you hold in your hand. What am I saying? You never know what connections will lead you to your destiny.

I was a featured guest on a local radio broadcast in Detroit where I shared a biblical perspective on the state of the family. I was invited back as a guest speaker to the Divorce Care Ministry that served me as I walked through my darkest days. I was able to see women sitting in the seats I sat in seven years prior, crying and broken. But this time, I was not the patient. I was there as an instrument of healing. I remember one woman in the group saying to me, "So, we're going to survive this?" I told her, "You will not only survive, but you will thrive if you hold on to God." They were able to see a woman now on the other side of the journey they were about to embark on. If I could make it, they could too.

Back to that powerful sermon. It had so many "golden nuggets", it was as if it were designed just for me. It was enlightening and revelatory. In the message, a distinction was made between scars and wounds. The pastor stated that survivors have wounds, but overcomers have scars. It was easy for me to connect that statement to my own experience. When I was in survival mode, I was deeply wounded and hurting from my divorce experiences. The slightest irritation would cause additional pain because my wounds were fresh, still open. However, as God brought healing to my life, my wounds began to close up and they were no longer sensitive to the slightest irritation. As the healing process continued over several years, the wounds closed completely and today, only a scar remains. The scar is necessary because it is a reminder of what I went through. I need to remember because when I view my life in its current blessed state, I get overwhelmed with emotion as I recount what it took to get here. The scar is a reminder of the work God did in my life and the hope that has been restored.

I am often asked will I marry again. I honestly do not know the answer to that question. I am not opposed to it and still believe it is God's gift to humanity. I am blessed to have wholesome examples around me that encourage me and remind me that beautiful relationships are indeed possible. I am in a good place in my life and have discovered true fulfillment as a single woman. That does not mean I wish to remain single for the rest of my days, but I am maximizing this season of life and if by chance I am found by a man that realizes he has discovered a jewel of great price, well...we shall see.

I am a witness that God wastes nothing. Every tear was a wet prayer. Every prayer was an act of faith. Every act of faith was an opportunity for God to move in my life. Today, I am a soon-to-be college grad (with high honors), executing my plan to retire from the University of Michigan in the near future, and looking forward to my next assignment as a social worker. I have been approached about hosting a radio broadcast and contacted about serving my community as a potential member on the Board Directors for a Christian Health Organization. Oh yes! We can now add to my list of accomplishments, PUBLISHED AUTHOR.

TO GOD BE THE GLORY FOR THE THINGS HE HAS DONE!

References

"What is trauma", 2. (2019, May 6). *What is Trauma.* Retrieved from Center for Anxiety Disorders: https://centerforanxietydisorders.com/what-is-trauma/

Custody and parenting time . (2019, May 13). Retrieved from Michigan Legal Help: https://michiganlegalhelp.org/self-help-tools/family/custody-and-parenting-time#

Forgiveness. (2019, May 14). *Forgiveness: Your Health Depends on it.* Retrieved from Johns Hopkins Medicine: https://www.hopkinsmedicine.org/health/wellness-and-prevention/forgiveness-your-health-depends-on-it

Harris, R. C. (2013). Coronary artery bypass grafting. *Annals of Cardiothoracic Surgery*, 579.

Huurre, T. J. (2006). Long-term psychosocial effects of parental divorce . *European Archives of Psychiatry and Clinical Neuroscience* , 256-263.

Manning-Schaffel, V. (2018, December 5). *What is codependency? Signs of a codependent relationship* . Retrieved from NBC News : https://www.nbcnews.com/better/health/what-codependency-signs-codependent-relationship-ncna940666

Redeem, D. o. (2019, May 13). *Definition of redeem* . Retrieved from Merriam Webster : https://www.merriam-webster.com/dictionary/redeem

Selva, J. (2018, August 22). *Codependency: What are the signs and how to overcome it*. Retrieved from Positive Psychology Program : https://positivepsychologyprogram.com/codependency-definition-signs-worksheets/#signs-codependency

www.ingramcontent.com/pod-product-compliance
Lightning Source LLC
LaVergne TN
LVHW091557060526
838200LV00036B/879